# HELP! THERE'S A CHILD IN MY CHURCH!

# HELP! THERE'S A CHILD IN MY CHURCH!

## Working with 7-11s

### PETER GRAYSTONE

Scripture Union
130 City Road, London EC1V 2NJ

For Paul, whom I love
something chronic.

## Acknowledgements

Cover design and artwork — Mark Carpenter.
Cover photography — Steve Shipman.
Inside artwork — Neil Pinchbeck.

© Peter Graystone 1989

First published 1989
Reprinted 1990

British Library Cataloguing in Publication Data

Graystone, Peter
  Help! There's a child in my church!
  1. Sunday Schools
  I. Title
  268′.43

ISBN 0 86201 544 8

Printed and bound in Great Britain by
Cox and Wyman, Ltd, Reading.

# Contents

# Foreword

Pudsey Bear, the 'Children in Need' mascot, was arrested last week at my local railway station. He had travelled hundreds of miles, apparently without a ticket. The unfortunate stuffed bear pleaded his innocence and local residents raised over a thousand pounds to bail him out. Pudsey's vast, smiling bulk appeared on the BBC television appeal after all.

'Children in Need' annually touches the hearts—and the wallets—of millions of people. We *care* about children when their needs are obvious. But *every* child has needs.

This book is for all those who care about the children who rarely hit the headlines—the children we see in our churches and those whom we would like to see there.

Those who work with children in groups like Sunday or weeknight clubs, the Sunday 'school'—a name and a model that are rightly moving out of use—or in uniformed organizations will find here an abundance of practical help. But we must not *restrict* children to being always with others of the same narrow age-band. Every generation needs the others. Adults need children as well as children needing adults. So I'd like this book to be read by all who care about the wholeness of the church 'family'.

Every child needs to feel valued by and of significance to

that 'family'. Yes, the thinking and the practices described in this book are primarily about the way that children develop and learn, and how this affects a *group* of children working together. But that thinking also needs to be reflected in the total life of any church which includes children. (No children in your church? Then are there none in the local community?)

Jesus Christ himself told us not to exclude children, but to learn from them (Mark 10:13–16). He said that we welcome *him* into our midst when we welcome a child in his name (Mark 9:36–37). How then can we say, 'The children in my church are someone else's responsibility'?

Of course, many of us would be more welcoming to children if our first thought were not, '*Help*! There's a child in my church!' The boisterous child *is* alarming to the older person with arthritis. The noisy child *can* be seen as causing a disturbance. And if we have not talked to a child in years, we may indeed feel at a loss. Well, here's a book to help our understanding and remove much of the alarm and anxiety. We might become a warmer, richer fellowship after reading these pages. Some of us might even volunteer to help with a children's group, perhaps once a month, or for a six-month trial period. Few will volunteer if there is no experienced help at hand, nobody in the church with a training role, nobody who can help the beginner to understand children, to develop story-telling and questioning skills, to make use of drama and craft, to lead children in worship, to make visual aids, and so on. Here is a book that will do that— especially if the reader works through the questions and things to do at the end of each chapter. And some of this help is needed by those who lead intergenerational worship, learning and fun activities.

There are children in need of God's good news right across our land. Some gather in our church halls. Some are worshipping with the church family, at least on occasions. Some live next door to church members or just down the road.

God's kingdom is wide open to children. Is your church?

**Margaret V. Old**

7

# 1
## It's a waist-high world

I like children! There is no point in disguising that fact, because it would have emerged sooner or later. I like the things they bring into church life — their straightforward response to Jesus, their spontaneity, their need to enjoy themselves in God's presence.

An example! I had been speaking at an all-age service where the whole congregation, adults and children, had worshipped together. I was standing on the church steps, shaking hands with people in the traditional way. Victoria, three years old, marched up to me and stared me straight in the eye. She lifted her skirts high above her head and declared, 'Look Peter, new knickers!'

Now this was a new experience for me in the established church! It certainly doesn't happen much among the adult congregation! But it does illustrate something important about the way children approach church. There are, for children, no preconceptions about what is 'the right thing to do'. It is we adults who learn to put church in a special compartment, different from anything else that happens to

*'Look Peter, new knickers!'*

us. Children simply accept it as another of life's rich variety of experiences.

Ten-year-old Raju, grin stretching from ear to ear after playing football in the car park, sees no reason to change his expression just because he has walked into a church building — it's me who has learnt to put on a 'Sunday' face as soon as I start to pray. Seven-year-old Clare, who leaps around like a rattlesnake when she gets excited, has no qualms about clapping, bouncing and singing full blast in her enthusiasm to praise God's greatness — it is the church's pianist who looks at her wistfully, wondering where he got his adult inhibitions from.

On the other hand, three-year-old Caroline, who is scared of unfamiliar buildings and hates being left without her dad, does not find it easier to be left in the Sunday School than the council playgroup. The fact that she is among God's people, who love her, means nothing to her until they have proved it. And Mark, who is thirteen and loathes singing because it gives away the fact that his voice is beginning to break, finds no consolation whatever in the fact that hymns are sung for God, not for those around him. As far as he is concerned, a grunt and a squeak sound just as bad in the church as in the bath.

There is a principle here, and it is an important one. The way in which we are most effectively going to help children discover the truth about the Kingdom of God is to start right where they are! The wrong approach is to consider everything that adult Christians know, then work out how to prod and push children until they know it all as well. The right approach is to consider what the children are familiar with, and help them to take step after step forward from there in an increasing understanding of and response to God. The wrong approach is to expect children to put up with experiences which they would not have anywhere else — long sermons, complicated theological words, extended periods of sitting still and quiet — no matter how right and precious these things are for adult Christians. The right approach is to consider what activities make the children feel comfortable — things they enjoy at clubs, exciting ways of learning at school — and use those to bring glory to God.

Joan King, Scripture Union's families' adviser, speaks of 'salami-sliced children' chopped up by some churches according to age, sex and background, with spiritual life kept separate from all the other slices of day-to-day life. But God is God of the whole sausage!

## Jesus' example

Of course, none of this carries any weight unless it is backed up by the authority of Jesus' example and the Bible's teaching. If Jesus made no concessions to children, then there is no point in reading any further.

In fact, the value that Jesus placed upon children is even more striking than one might imagine it to be. Remember that the culture of the children who met Jesus was very different from ours. In today's society, children have a high profile — television programmes are made specially for them, laws exist specifically to protect them, fashions are designed for them in particular. However in first century Hebrew society children were placed quite low in the order of priority.

Certainly there was no question of them being active participants in God's worship. In the synagogue, children under
twelve and all women were consigned to a gallery. They
were kept separate from the adult men who dominated the
proceedings as Yahweh, the covenant God, our God, was
praised and his Law taught. This is the religious life that
Jesus would have known for his first twelve years — allowed
only to be an observer at the worship of his own Father.

When children approached Jesus, his disciples turned
them away (Mark 10:13–16). They were not being cruel,
they were simply doing what any responsible disciples would
do for a Jewish rabbi. After all, the place for boys was
synagogue-school, the place for girls was the home! In that
context, Jesus' words and actions were surprising, maybe
even shocking: 'Let the children come to me and do not stop
them, because the Kingdom of God belongs to such as these.'
I imagine that there was amazement for some and delight
for others as Jesus took the children in his arms and gave
each an individual blessing.

It is interesting to note what Jesus did not do! He didn't
tell the children Bible stories, although he must have known
them, and he didn't give them any profound theological
teaching. He just loved them! I suppose that, knowing their
background of passive obedience to the teacher-rabbi, and
virtual exclusion from worship, he was giving them precisely
what they needed most at that point of their development —
the love of an adult man, and the unquestioning welcome of
God himself. He was starting right where they were, with
things they could understand and an experience they may
well never have forgotten. It was the adults who got the strict
talking to!

## Following the example

The love of Christian adults should also be the first experience that our children are aware of in church. Children who
are taken to church in their first months of life do not need
to hear Bible stories or learn theological truths. The first
things they need to learn about God are that in a church,

among God's people, they will be cared for and kept safe. That's not to say that Bible stories are unimportant — but they can be kept for a while until they match the needs and capability of a child. Don't underestimate, though, what a child can learn about God before his or her first birthday. The baby who finds the church to be a warm building where she can sleep when she needs to, then find bright colours and interesting people to engage her attention when she needs that, is not merely being kept amused, but is learning that love and protection are characteristics of God. But the baby who discovers that the church is the place where he is allowed to lie wet without his nappy changed, or be kept in distress because his mother or father is not nearby, is learning negative things about God which may stay with him subconsciously for many years.

It would be a mistake to imagine that this applies only to very young children. It is easy to persuade yourself that the thing a nine-year-old child needs most to learn on a freezing Sunday in winter as the wind hurtles past the window is the significance of the hygiene and health regulations in Leviticus. If we are to follow Jesus' approach and start at the point of the child's greatest need, it may be more appropriate to begin with a game of 'Chain He'. This is not just a matter of entertaining children — at a deep level they are learning things about God through his caring representatives on Earth. They will arrive at the point where they are warmer and full of excitement — in a much better condition to continue worshipping God and to learn from the Bible. They will discover that God is concerned about their fitness, their comfort, their happiness, their skills — not just their 'souls'. Come to think of it, isn't that what the health and hygiene regulations in Leviticus are all about?

Not enough room for 'Chain He'? Oh come on — use your imagination! How about on-the-spot aerobics, or some action songs? It's not even against the law to go to the park! It's a waist-high world! Try asking yourself, 'If I were four, or nine, or twelve, what would I *love* to do on a Sunday morning?' Then think about how you could use those activities — craft, games, collecting, acting, dressing up or whatever — to share the good news of Jesus' salvation.

## What about the Bible?

A worthwhile Sunday School needs to be child-centred. But equally importantly, every Sunday School needs to be Bible-based. From the very first moments that God made his plans for mankind available in written form, he has been concerned that children should have access to them. Immediately after Moses had received God's ten commandments, inscribed in stone, he passed on this message, 'The LORD ... is our God. Love the LORD your God with all your heart, with all your soul and with all your strength. Never forget these commands that I am giving you today. *Teach them to your children*. Repeat them when you are at home and when you are away, when you are resting and when you are working' (Deuteronomy 6:4–7). People who mean business with God have always taken these words seriously. Paul reminded the young Timothy how central they had been in his life: 'Continue in the truths that you were taught and firmly believe. You know who your teachers were, and you remember that *ever since you were a child, you have known the Holy Scriptures*, which are able to give you the wisdom that leads to salvation through faith in Jesus Christ' (2 Timothy 3:14–15).

Both of these passages are challenging to Sunday School leaders — and also to parents, because the responsibility for teaching children to love and obey God is given unambiguously to them. In Timothy's case we know that he learned faith in God from his grandmother Lois and his mother Eunice, but we also know of the debt he owed to Paul, who taught him, prayed for him and enabled him to come alive to everything that God wanted to do with his life (2 Timothy 1:6). There will be more to think about later on when we look at how Sunday School leaders and parents share the responsibility for the Christian nurture of children.

So we need never settle for children's work that responds only to children's recreational needs. To maintain a programme which merely offers children love and enjoyment while 'the adults get on with real business of worshipping God' is missing the point. The search is on for a scheme of activities which is thoroughly child-centred, dealing with the needs and joys of a child at any particular age, but also rooted in the discovery and application of the Bible and the worship of God.

## A church without children?

A church without children is a poor church. It is like the childless 'Chitty Chitty Bang Bang' village! There is a much-quoted phrase, 'Today's child is tomorrow's church.' Well . . . yes and no! It is true that our Sunday Schools are caring for the next generation of mature Christians and that to enter adulthood with a broad, basic knowledge of Bible truths is a valuable privilege. But it is also true that today's children are today's church! Unless we wish to disagree with Jesus' declaration that 'the Kingdom of God belongs to such as these', we need to give children the very same status and prominence as adults in our churches — now! And if we take seriously Jesus' warning, 'Whoever does not receive the Kingdom of God like a child will never enter it', then we have some important learning from children to do. That cannot happen unless adults and children meet, mix and worship together. Our churches cannot manage without children — not because of the pleasure they bring, but because of what they have to teach us about God.

Now there's a thought to take your hat off to!

### Things to do

**1** Make a list of all the activities which take place formally in your church — or, at least, all the ones you know of! Include Sunday services, regular activities such as a choir or midweek

15

groups, social events, work the church does in the community and all children's groups. Put them in three columns:

| Those which are for children only (except for their adult/leaders) | Those which are usually for adults | Those at which adults and children are both welcome |
|---|---|---|
| | | |

**2** Underline in red all those activities which help with the spiritual needs of those involved.

Next, underline in blue all those which help with physical needs — it does not matter if this means underlining some twice.

Finally, underline in another colour all those which are concerned with social or emotional needs.

**3** Now examine the results:
(a) Are the activities reasonably well distributed among the three columns?
(b) Do all three underlining colours appear in every column?
(c) Thinking particularly of the children in the age-group for which you are concerned, does the list reveal any shortcomings in what your church provides?

**4** Pray about the thoughts you have had while making the list, thanking God for what is good and asking him to allow improvements to take place in what is lacking. Decide to whom you could talk about the results as the first stage in reacting to them.

# 2

## It wasn't like that in my day

I'm not sure that it's correct to say, 'Kids never change!' We probably all agree that the world in which children live is changing rapidly — and I think it is true that, as it changes, it pushes children into a new mould in each generation. It's not necessarily a worse world, but it is a different one from the world which most Sunday School leaders knew when they were seven.

## An accelerating world

Children are being encouraged to see themselves as mature at a progressively younger age. Whoever heard of ten-year-old girls wearing make up in the 1970s? Or of boys needing to be sure that every tiny detail of their clothes matched that year's fashion? The reason for it is that manufacturers have realized that there are big bucks to be had in introducing pre-teenagers to the pop culture. You can love it or lament it, but you cannot ignore it or blame children for it!

The nature of family life is changing rapidly too. Almost every child in the country now has a friend who does not live with both his natural parents, or is in that situation himself. That is sad, but a child is not committing a sin if he cannot bounce into church with both father and mother. Communities are changing as families move more often from one part of the country to another. Whatever the colour of a child's skin, he or she is likely to live in close proximity to children who have skin of a different colour. Even if they mix infrequently, local schools will be aware of the variety of religions and cultures represented in the area. Most of them respond in the only way possible — by developing a religious education syllabus which is relevant to all those in their catchment area. The practical result of this is that most children know a tiny amount about several religions, without being able to distinguish them, and without necessarily seeing Christianity as distinct.

Schools are changing in other ways too. The serried ranks of desks, at which children sat silently listening to wisdom being dispensed, have given way to tables, around which children explore, discover and discuss the important things of life. This has meant that far fewer children are condemned to school-years of bored incomprehension. More learn to read than ever before. More can handle money and basic arithmetic than ever before. More can express their point of view than ever before. Where previously children copied a diagram of a growing leaf from the blackboard, now they will have several plants in front of them on the table, and will measure them, weigh them, experiment on them, draw them, write poems about them and discuss their results together. Primary education has become, on the whole, more enjoyable and fulfilling, with less children emerging as failures from the system. If a Sunday School persists in offering the 'you listen, I talk' approach, it risks losing the children's interest, then losing the children's good will, then losing the children.

There are new excitements and opportunities in the children's world. They have the chance to share previously unimaginable experiences through television, to grow up in good health, to take holidays abroad and to spend pocket money on a huge variety of tempting pleasures.

However, the accelerating world has brought dangers with

it too. The decay of city centres and the fragmentation of rural communities have meant that the difference between those who enjoy the benefits described in the previous paragraph and those who do not is wider than ever before. Among those children who are trapped in areas of poor housing, bad debt, high unemployment and frequent crime, there is a growing sense of injustice that others have come to accept a high standard of living as a right. Among those children who experience a good deal of security and what was once luxury, there is usually ignorance of the fact that others living nearby do not have the same privileges. It is tempting to identify spiritual dangers for children who missed out on the new prosperity, but comfort brings dangers with it too. While the widening divide goes on hurting the nation's children, no Sunday School leader can be complacent about it.

Churches also need to be aware of the growing incidence of abuse of children in all kinds of ways. The possibility of physical and sexual abuse or emotional neglect needs to be tucked away in the conscious mind of all those who work with children. Am I right in saying that the incidence of these is growing, or are we simply more aware now of what was once covered up as a guilty secret? Whichever is true, Sunday School leaders must open themselves to the unpalatable fact that the pressures which lead to people hurting children exist within churches as well as outside them.

It is also wise to add that the access to television and video, which has brought so many valuable things into the lives of children, has been bought at a price. It has brought knowledge in wonderful ways, but it has also brought knowledge of the world's violence, of corruption, of sex, and the hidden influences of advertising and of secular morality presented as a norm. None of these things are dangerous in themselves — they simply leave behind them the nagging fear that one day we may regret that we let children find out so much about the adult world so soon. Maybe!

# How should we react?

A Sunday School leader cannot fight the onward march of the world single-handed! It may well be that he or she will want to pray and work for change in the structure of the country, but the first priority in the Sunday School is to give individual children the means to cope with the world in which they live.

As well as explaining Christian values and living them as an example, it is important to avoid saying or doing things which put obstacles in the way of children. Do not pass judgment on the way children dress or the music and films which influence them. No matter how much you personally like or dislike boys with earrings or girls in clothes that are meant to flaunt an allure which they do not yet possess, these things have to be seen in the context of the pressures children are under.

Try to be careful with the words you use. Teach yourself to avoid saying, 'Take this letter home to your mother and father' or, 'Why don't you help Mum with the washing up?' by putting yourself in the shoes of a child whose mother has died or lives in another house. Use the expression 'the grown ups at home' instead — that way you are not unintentionally reprimanding a child for not having a standard nuclear family.

Be aware of what is happening in schools and children's television. Talk about those of different religions in a way which encourages friendship and respect, but points out that Christianity is unique. The majority of Christians in the world are black, so avoid giving the impression that to follow Jesus one needs to be white and live in the suburbs. Choose illustrations and stories which show Christian children from a variety of races and with different colours of skin.

Above all, make sure that you know the children in your care, and that you are in touch with the world they live in. Don't tell them it is a terrible world — don't even think it! It is a fallen world, but the men and women in it are unspeakably precious to God. They are capable of being great because of what Jesus has done, and the children in it can 'shine like stars in the universe as you hold out the word of life' (Philippians 2:15 NIV).

## What are children like?

Am I making a mistake in writing this chapter? Maybe! I am aware that no two children are alike, so perhaps I am asking for trouble in trying to pin down characteristics which all children in a seven to eleven age-range share. It is tremendously important to know each of the children you work with as an individual. There are many children of seven (and, frankly, some adults) who have not developed emotionally beyond five. I was aware of this recently when a once-off visitor to our Sunday School hid her head under her mother's coat and refused to tell me her name. Her younger sister, who was four, going on twenty-five, breezed in like a debutante, helped herself to crayons and a seat and announced, 'Don't worry about Jenny. She's always like this. Have you got anything for me to colour?'

Equally, there are eleven-year-old children who have developed physically beyond their peers. It is not unusual to have one or two girls in a group who have shot up in height, and anything which makes them embarrassed about it should be avoided. Neither is there anything especially unusual for some boys of this age to be moody occasionally or sexually curious — they are just growing up faster than average. However, I can't help noticing that some characteristics are shared by many children at this stage of their lives, so it is probably worth listing them.

### Full of energy

To ask a child to sit in one place for a long time is to ask the impossible. All the energy will simply turn itself into a restless need to fidget or disrupt. Provide chances to be active, a variety of fast-moving experiences, and the opportunity to take part in what is going on. There is no point in fighting a child's natural energy. Provide ways of using it enjoyably instead.

## Eager to learn

In the months before I flew to Malta on a holiday with my godson, he developed a craze for aeroplanes. In a staggeringly short space of time he had read every book on them in the library. With one glance towards the clouds he could identify an aircraft and tell me the serial number, the make of the engine, the seating capacity and the colour of the hostess' eye-shadow, while I was still trying to work out whether I was looking at an aircraft or a bird.

These crazes are a chance for the child to share information or a new skill with the leader, so be open to allowing them to teach you something, and take an interest. Also, use this eagerness to learn as a way of interesting children in the Bible. I was studying Nehemiah with a group who suddenly latched on to the fact that the walls of Jerusalem had a special gate used solely for getting rid of sewage. I was happy to let them read about this for a few minutes because the story had suddenly come alive to them as one about real people who had real lives and needed to get rid of their refuse just as surely as we do. Whether the point that I wanted to make from the story came across with the same impact is not important — the learning which mattered on that occasion was that the events of the Bible relate to life today.

Alongside this thirst for information comes a desire to define what is 'real'. For the first time, children develop the ability to distinguish between truth and fantasy, and the distinction between the two becomes very important. The fact that what they hear about the life of Jesus is, in every sense, the truth, can deeply impress children. However, miracle stories can present a problem to them, so it is wise to stress the purpose of the miracles — powerful acts of love by the very same God who cares for us today — rather than to present them as fantastic acts of wizardry.

## Heroes and heroines

A happy child's life is usually full of adventure. Along the side of the garden in which I spent every sunny day of my first eight years was a tunnel covered over with dense laburnum trees. Down that tunnel I was chased by Batman day after day as I made my escape on my trusty four-wheel-drive donkey, Neddy. I never got caught and am sure that consistently playing the villain for years on end has irreparably damaged my psyche. (Incidentally, I was searching through the attic recently and discovered that Neddy was actually a dog. I can't think why I never noticed before!)

We can present the Bible as a succession of heroes and heroines, and the life of a Christian as one of adventure. Jesus was a unique hero, and a real one — but a different kind of hero. His followers do not renounce excitement when they commit themselves to his lifstyle — they start a huge challenge. Acting out the stories of Bible heroes helps children to identify with them, and seeing their leaders follow an adventurous lifestyle offers a role-model. Very often children find their own hero and heroine figures from among their leaders. This is a great opportunity which can be used to point them to God, but it brings daunting responsibilities with it as well. It is also good to tell children about the lives of heroic Christians in the history of the church, being careful to include the stories of great Christian women, which are not aired so often.

## Down to earth

Children do not think in abstract ways until they are in their teens. Knowing this, we need to be careful that the words we use convey what we intend them to mean. Any boy will tell you that 'being saved' is what happens to footballs on their way to the goal post, not to Christians on their way to the Kingdom of God. Just as bad is the tendency to use phrases which carry no meaning at all. 'Being faithful to God' is a meaningless expression to a child, but it can be explained by examples ('Suppose everyone told you that you were stupid to be a friend to God, but you refused to break friends with him ever because he meant so much to you. . . .').

Hymns and antiquated Bible translations are notorious for provoking confusion. Antonia was pushing her luck when she rushed up to me declaring, 'James just said sod.'

'You're allowed to,' grinned James. 'The vicar said it in church.'

'Whatever are you talking about?' I asked.

'It's in "Good King Wenceslas". It rhymes with, "In his master's steps he trod!" '

We have never sung that carol since!

## Making things
Children are eagerly creative, and God made us to enjoy being creative. The Bible offers an endless stream of craftwork possibilities. This is too good a coincidence to miss!

## Justice and morality
These abstract words may not feature strongly in the children's vocabulary, but the words 'It's not fair' are almost certain to be used regularly. In a child's eyes, moral issues are usually 'right' or 'wrong', with no grey area between. The idea that wrong is either 'failing to get my own way' nor 'not doing what an adult says' slowly gives way to a more objective sense of morality as children grow towards their teens. It is at this age that they begin to realize the difference between 'being sorry' and 'saying sorry'. Because of this, the need for Jesus as a forgiving Saviour can begin to take on a significant meaning. The personal love and help of Jesus can come to play an important part in the lives of children who previously accepted it without much thought. It is a good age to encourage a 'natural' prayer life.

I remember an occasion when my mother came into my bedroom and found me sobbing. I said that it was because of a toothache, but it wasn't! It was because I had just read what happened to Joan of Arc and was crushed by the injustice of it all. I hope my mother reads this, because I never got around to apologizing for a wasted trip to the dentist. I am sure that the best way to help children of about seven to eleven to understand the significance of the crucifixion is to show them that it simply was not fair. Their natural sense of justice will tell them all they need to know in order to respond in an appropriate way.

## The gang

This can be very important to children who are decreasing in their dependence on adults and increasing in their desire to be 'in' with their peer group. In a Sunday School it is helpful to create a strong sense of group identity. Encourage children to cooperate with each other in craft-work or games, and involve them in simple decision-making as a group. You also need to be sensitive to anyone who has been left out of a gang — maybe because she is naturally a loner, maybe because he is not liked. Either way, the child will be aware of being excluded and will need special encouragement.

It may be that a girl is a slow learner and cannot keep up with the rest — in which case, make special provision for her to be helped when reading or writing is involved, and arrange activities in which she can show herself as skilful as the rest. It may be that a boy smells — in which case, ignore it and be more loving than ever. If insults are given, insist straightaway that you will not tolerate them, so that a group cannot gang up in opposition to an individual. Find virtues in the excluded boy to praise regularly.

The gang age is also the sex-segregated age. It is probably more trouble than it is worth to organize games or dances which involve the boys holding hands with girls. On the other hand, mixed groups for some activities, such as discussions or craft, mean that children can be helped to develop good attitudes to the opposite sex and prepare to treat them in a friendly and Christian way in adolescence. Single sex groups can sometimes become aggressive or spiteful and a mixture of boys and girls softens the extremes of behaviour shown by both.

As a teacher, I once decided to take on the sexism of the school, which allowed boys to choose between rounders and cricket, but allowed girls only rounders. There was bad feeling fermenting among the boys from the very moment I announced that cricket teams that afternoon would be mixed. When the match came, they made it clear that they were only doing what I had decided under duress. When one of the girls caught and bowled the boys' star player with her fourth attempt there was a near-riot. I paid for that decision

*'Owzat!'*

with a week's total non-cooperation from the boys. It was a nightmare!

But I don't regret it! I was only trying to see the children the way God knows them — not girls, not boys, not members of a gang, not scholars, not pre-teenagers, not numbers in a sociological grouping, not members of a race or nationality, not categorizable into neat packages. He just knows them by one wonderful Christian name after another.

## Things to do

**1** In a vertical column on the left hand side of a page, write down the seven characteristics of children identified in the second half of this chapter. Add any others which have occurred to you as you read, such as 'friendly' or 'talkative'.

Beside each characteristic, write the name of one or more children from your church who display it. Next to that, write down what you have seen them do which leads you to put those names there.

On the right hand side of the page, write some activities you

| Characteristic | Children | Observations | Response |
|---|---|---|---|
| Energy | Colin Emma | Disruptive during hymns | Songs with actions? Fewer? |
| Eager to learn | | | |
| Heroes | | | |
| Literal | | | |
| Creative | | | |
| Justice | | | |
| Gangs | | | |
| | | | |
| | | | |

could do in your Sunday School which would respond to those particular children's characteristics and promote their understanding of the Christian life at the same time.

2 Write down the names of any children who did not appear on the previous list because they do not comfortably fit the 'standard'. Every child is special and unique to God, but what makes these children special in particular? Do they find it easy to take part in the package of activities that your Sunday School offers, or should you provide different or extra activities to meet their needs?

3 Spend ten minutes in a toy shop and watch part of three or four children's television prgrammes (ask a child to help

you choose). Try to identify what it is about each toy or programme which makes it popular with children. Do the activities which you offer in Sunday School share any of the features that you identified as giving joy or fulfilment in the games or on the television?

# 3

## The old man with the white beard

Whatever we think God is like, we are always wrong! If we think we know how great he is, he is greater — otherwise he wouldn't be God. If we think we know how wise he is, he is wiser — that's part of the way we define God. With this in mind, it is clear that adults have got nothing to be smug about when they consider the way children understand God. Very often, children perceive things in a way which makes adults humble.

## How do children understand God?

I have just spent a superb day revisiting the school at which I used to teach. I had three questions I wanted to ask, 'What do you think God is like? What do you think Jesus is like? What do you think the Holy Spirit is like?' I chose to go to the ten-year-olds' class because I knew that, in this particular school in South London, the children would all have received a certain amount of Bible teaching by that age from their exceptional teacher, Joan Winton. I knew there would be no one who had not heard of God — I was interested in how they had interpreted the teaching they had received. The boys and girls represented a large range of abilities, and a wide variety of backgrounds — some from homes where Jesus is worshipped and followed, many where that is not the case.

Catherine gave me the most mature answers and I thought her understanding was as close to an adult's as it was possible to get. I haven't tampered with her spelling or grammar — why should I?

'God is wonderful and more powerful than anyone else. he answers our prays. He comes first in everything. He also comforts us and helps us to win through in the end.

'Jesus is just as wonderful and powerful as God. he gave his life for our sins it is him and God that we should believe in and be thankful for. He showed us his glory when he died for us and gave us the bible.

'The Holy Spirit is a bit like a ghost which lives in us but instead of it being a haunting ghost it is a loving one.'

In contrast, Kevin, who is the same age, thought this.

'God is like a man and has wite cloths on.

'Jesus is like a boy and has wite cloths like his dad.

'The Holy Spirit is like a ball of fire in the air.'

I was fascinated by his contrast between God as a man and Jesus as a boy. It made me realize how strongly children can identify with the young Jesus — perhaps we should make more of the few references we have to Jesus as a child. I imagine that, in trying to define the Holy Spirit, he is actually describing the sun. Consistently the children found this aspect of God the most difficult to grasp.

Sophie wrote about God as though he is a character in a fairy tale. If she were in my Sunday School, I would be anxious to make sure that, when she makes her 'attic clearance' of the childish things in her brain, she does not put God in the same refuse skip as dragons, goblins, and Father Christmas.

'God is like a King or a Mighty. Willing, helpful to others. Conqerer.

'Jesus is like a strong bold knight, willing to work like a slave.

'The Holy Spirit is like a wisp of smoke half man half angel who is willing to do as God commands.'

As a complete contrast, Helen's answers were fascinating. She was obviously trying to repeat the religious phrases that she had heard elsewhere, but she clearly learnt them without understanding them, because she hasn't quite got them right.

'I think God is like a man, but more powerful and wounderful than us.

'Jesus is like a dad to us all who died to save our sin. He love us and shares his glory.

'The Holy spirit is like God putting your granddads and relaitions into your heart and making you more like them.'

If she had written,'Jesus died to save us from the penalty of our sin', it would be recognizable as an adult's attempt to explain the mystery of how Jesus' death saves humans. As it is, she wrote, 'Jesus died to save our sin', which does not actually mean anything, but is evidently not a phrase that she came up with of her own accord. Even more interesting is the way Helen described the Holy Spirit in terms of the adults she respects. This is not at all unusual — but it makes Sunday School leaders hesitate, for it shows that children are judging God in terms of those humans who represent him. It is not a wrong thing for children to do — even Paul realized it would happen. At some points he urged his readers to follow Christ's example, but in 1 Corinthians 4:16, 17 he wrote, 'I urge you to imitate me. For this reason I am sending to you Timothy . . . who will remind you of my way of life in Christ Jesus.' Although children need to be encouraged to be like Jesus, it is their leaders' way of life which they will find it easier to understand.

And then there was the eccentric! Matthew wrote this.

'God. Very tall, white beard, halo, bible in his hand, very old he has a silver throne and all the angels are around him. He is very clever.

'Jesus. About 20 years old halo white cloths brown hair hand raised. Smileing. holding a cross in his hand. bare feet.

'Holy Spirit. A shining light in a ball of glass. It is sometimes a white dove with big eyes. The ball of glass is about as big as a football. God keeps it in a wooden box.'

Matthew, although he is the same age as the others, hasn't reached the stage where his mind can cope with abstract ideas. Every image is still concrete to him, so he didn't describe God in terms of love or justice — he described a statue of Jesus that he had seen. I have puzzled for some time as to what was in his mind when he described the Holy Spirit. The only clue I have is that in 'Transformers — the Movie' the life force which motivates the robots looks a bit like the glass ball he wrote about. There is a great deal of spiritual content in children's films of the last five years. I don't mean Christian content — I mean a vague sort of spiritual significance to events and characters. It is, maybe, a sign that although children and adults are taught less about the religious part of their nature, the need which God put inside them to respond to something more than food, money and sex has not gone away. Perhaps it began in the early 1980s when millions who had not been to church for years found inspiration in the death, resurrection and ascension of 'ET — the extra-terrestrial'. If only they had known that the story was a rip-off from a true one in the Bible.

## Helping children understand more

There is nothing wrong with children thinking of God as an ancient, bearded man in the clouds — it is all their minds can cope with. However, it would be sad if they reached adulthood still thinking that there is nothing more to God than that. The Sunday School leader's job is to move the children gently forward in their understanding, never forgetting that it is the Holy Spirit at work in children who gives them greater spiritual perception, not any human.

Understanding God is a tough problem. However, it was not humans who first identified the problem, it was God himself! That is one of the reasons he sent Jesus, the complete expression of God in human form. It is a great deal easier to understand Jesus than it is to understand the invisible, omniscient Creator — and understanding Jesus is the best place to start when helping children to find out about God. The more we can portray Jesus as a real person (not a mythical figure), in a particular time and place (not a white, middle-class Englishman who happened to wear robes), who was unique because he was God (not just good, not magical, but divine), the closer children will get to the truth. It is by marvelling at Jesus' actions that children will begin to sense God's awesome power, and by hearing about the way peoples' lives were changed after they met Jesus, that they will glimpse God's holiness.

Of course, there are other features of Christianity that children need to know as well, but it is best to root these in concrete terms. For example, rather than explaining faith in God in abstract terms, children can be shown what faith meant practically to Abraham, to Paul, to any one of the Bible's cast of thousands, and also to present-day adults whom they know. When they need to know the basic truth that God is the Creator, it will help them to examine parts of his creation with their own eyes and hands. The sense of wonder and awe which we long for them to discover will grow far stronger through their own experience than through listening to someone's explanation. And when it becomes important to deal with a part of the Bible which is not in story-form (maybe a part of an epistle, or the warnings of a prophet), a modern, fictional story or parable can illustrate the Biblical truth in a far more effective way than bare teaching.

A leader's role in helping children to understand God is a delicate combination of giving practical and biblical teaching, correcting wrong ideas in a sympathetic way, and trusting the Holy Spirit rather than expecting too much too soon. I remember an occasion when, after giving what I thought was an exemplary, short explanation of God's guidance, I asked a group how they thought God might show them what to do. A young boy answered, 'Perhaps he could send a little fairy to whisper in your ear.' There was a groan of derision from some of the older children and a look of panic spread across the boy's face as he realized he had said something wrong. At the time I thought it was more important to discipline the children who were insulting him and rebuild his confidence in himself, than to show him he was wrong. I came back to the subject on a subsequent occasion and tried to speak in even simpler terms. As years have gone by, I have seen the boy's comprehension grow clearer. There was no need to rush and risk confusing him or, worse still, make him think that his way of understanding was not good enough for God.

People have asked me, 'How can I teach the concept of the Trinity to my children? It's impossible for them to grasp!' In reply I can only wonder why those children need to be told something that is impossible for them to grasp! They can wait for that until later on. There is so much for them to be excited or challenged about that they *can* understand.

One of the children who answered my questions about Jesus wrote, 'I think if he could die for me on a cross he's Pretty Great. I think he is super (he's my hero).' Theologically, that is an inadequate explanation of Jesus, but in terms of a ten-year-old's response to the truth she had discovered, I think it is wonderful. In fact, it has an excitement about it that, after years of writing about Christ and expounding the Bible, I sometimes think I have lost. For a split second, I thought Laura understood Jesus better than I did. But it didn't last long!

## Letting children respond

Three factors help children's understanding of God to mature. The first is the concern of an adult, be it a parent or a Sunday School leader, that it should do so. The second is a wide exposure to the content of the Bible, and later chapters will help leaders to take a significant role in this. The third is the natural human process of growing up — and over that church leaders have no control whatever, since it will happen whether they like it or not!

It is good to allow children to express what they think of God at every stage of their lives. It will not always be a full understanding, but it is unhelpful to tell a child dogmatically that he has a wrong understanding simply because his thinking has not yet developed enough.

I was once surrounded by a group of boys, slouching on the floor in my living room, reading the closing chapter of

*'Wow, I'm going to do back flips.'*

the Bible. One of them said to me, 'Peter, when it says that there will be no more pain in heaven, does it mean that you can't hurt yourself there?'

'Yes, I think it probably does.'

'Wow!' he responded with a broad grin. 'I'm going to do back-flips!'

It was an absolutely perfect response to God's promise by a child of that age. Of course, it was way short of the full understanding of eternal life that will be revealed in heaven, but it was none the less acceptable for that. An adult could never have enthused over the prospect in the same way. Mind you, now he has put the idea in my head, I can't wait to get there and have a try!

## Things to do

**1** In five separate sections, write down all the things which you think it is important for children in this age-range to find out . . .

(a)  about God the Father.
(b)  about Jesus.
(c)  about the Holy Spirit.
(d)  about the church.
(e)  about the Bible.

**2**  Next to each fact, write down one part of the Bible which you could use with the children so that they will learn about it. It may be a Bible story, but don't forget that you could also include prophecy, psalms, epistles, parts of the Law, and so on.

**3**  Think back over what you have covered recently with the children in the Sunday School. Have you missed out anything that was on your list? Have any of the stories you have told had little to do with the facts you have decided you want children to discover? (For example, does the story of Samson help children of this age to find out any of the things you listed?)

**4**  Ask the children in your group to answer these questions, either orally or in writing:
(a)  What is God like?
(b)  What is Jesus like?
(c)  What is the Holy Spirit like?
When you have thought about their answers, pray for each child individually, asking God to help you to help them.

# 4
# But Mum, what's church for?

I have been fortunate enough to visit many churches — sometimes to give training or Bible teaching, sometimes to watch and join in what is happening. I started off trying not to push churches into categories — nothing is as simple as that. However, they seem to have pushed themselves into categories in my memory without my even asking, so you will have to accept that I don't mean these to appear so cut and dried as they do in print.

## Four models for the role of children in churches

There are strengths and weaknesses to all of the four models that follow.

### The obstacle course

In the first model, the children's work of the church is quite separate from the worship and teaching of the adult congregation. The function of the Sunday School is to evangelize and convert children, and it is only after such a programme of instruction that they are able to take their

place among the adults. Before reaching the door of the main section of the church, children will have vaulted across the hurdle called teaching, squeezed under the tarpaulin called evangelism and leapt through the hoop called conversion. The members of the church might well say, 'Our children's work is very important because it keeps the children usefully occupied while the adults get on with the real business of the church — worshipping and serving God.'

## Little Junior

In the second model, the Sunday School is highly valued, but functions completely separately from the adult congregation. They both take worship and teaching very seriously, but they never meet. At some point in their development, children are promoted from the 'junior' church to the 'adult' church. The congregation might say, 'Our children's work is very important because, after all, today's child is tomorrow's

church.' Incidentally, many Sunday Schools name themselves
'Junior Church', but it does not necessarily follow that they
adopt this pattern. I have long since ceased to judge church
work by its title — I went happily for many years to a youth
club called 'Eutychus' before realizing that it was named
after a New Testament character who fell asleep at a religious
meeting!

### The hide-and-seek church
The third model attempts to reach and cater for the children
of the area who have no connection at all with a church.

Sometimes the association between the children's work and the church is not immediately obvious, because there is a high emphasis on social and physical needs. It is only when you realize that Christians are staffing and providing the facilities for the children that you understand where the church fits in. The church leaders might say, with a lot of wisdom, 'Our children's work is very important because it allows the church to address the needs of the most needy — not just easy targets.'

### Learning together

Model four sees children as a part of the church on entirely equal terms with adults. Sometimes children and adults will worship and learn together, sometimes they will be separate and have activities appropriate to their own ages. Adults of the church might say, 'Our children's work is very important because today's child can be today's Christian. How are children going to learn from adults unless they join them in

worship and recreation? How are adults going to learn from children if they are kept separate?'

## Choosing a model

Let me say straightaway that, being as greedy as I am, I want the best of all four approaches for the children I know. I want them to come to a state of devoted commitment to God, which is the emphasis of model one. I want them to be able to learn about God at a level that is suited precisely to them, which model two can provide. I want churches to pay attention to the many children who cannot even begin to take part in traditional church life because nothing in their culture has prepared them for it, and, in many areas, visionary Christians are using model three very effectively as a witness to

41

children whom other churches have conveniently forgotten. (Those who run children's work in this kind of situation where, for example, local children may not even get out of bed on a Sunday morning, will need to look at a specialist book when they have finished this one.) However, the model which I would like to see embracing the strengths of all the others is the last one. Why? Because there seems to be a demand for it in the Bible.

The major indication in Jesus' ministry that he placed a uniquely high value on children was his intervention in an argument among his disciples (Mark 9:33–37). Their quarrel was over which of them was greatest. Jesus responded by placing a child among the adults and suggesting that the disciples thought about this action if they wanted to understand the true nature of greatness. Jesus seemed to be doing more than advocating humility. He said that those who welcomed children, welcomed him. The disciples would begin to understand the Kingdom of God only when they saw the child and the adult alongside one another.

Without the child, the adult could not and cannot fully understand God. This is even more telling in Matthew's account of the incident (18:1–5). He quotes Jesus as saying that God has revealed to children things which adults cannot comprehend (11:25).

This is in dramatic contrast to the role that children had previously played in Hebrew society. The overwhelming majority of references to children in the Old Testament are to their duties — to obey and respect parents (Deuteronomy 21:18–21), to pay attention without question (Proverbs 1:8), to accept being told off (Proverbs 13:1), to become educated (Proverbs 28:7), to be seriously aware of impending age (Ecclesiastes 12:1) and so on. There is no such catalogue of responsibilities in the other direction, although fathers are told to teach discipline. Having children is unmistakably a mark of status — Psalms 127 and 128 are explicitly concerned with the blessings that being a parent (of a son) brings.

You will remember that in the synagogue there was a pattern of exclusion until the age of twelve, when boys (but

again, not girls) were considered old enough to be participants. Until then, they were merely trainees, learning by
chanting, repetition and committing Scripture to memory. It
is almost recognizable as our model one, in which children
wait until maturity before they can express their standing in
God.

So when Jesus said that adults need children (he did not
distinguish between boys and girls) for practical reasons as
well as prestige, it was a breakthrough. From our viewpoint,
we can see that it harked back to examples in the Old
Testament. It is interesting to notice that the young Samuel
served God before synagogue worship excluded children like
him. It was a time when 'there were very few messages from
the Lord' (1 Samuel 3:1). When God needed to reprove the
people of Israel, he spoke to a child in the middle of the
night. Not surprisingly, Samuel was so conditioned to obey
adults without question that he immediately assumed that
Eli, the priest, required something of him. It was to Eli's
credit that he finally recognized God's part in it, and told
Samuel how to listen to God in prayer. Then it was the child
who taught the adult, not the other way round.

As we read of the early church establishing itself in the
years after Jesus' resurrection, there are a few clues to suggest
that children took more part in church life. The apostles
baptized whole households — children, relations, slaves,
all — when the head of the household was converted. Thus,
when the jailer at Philippi turned to Christ, all his family
were baptized with him (Acts 16:33). When Peter baptized
Cornelius, all his relatives joined him (Acts 10:48). This was
a direct link back to the covenants that God made with Noah,
Abraham and Moses in the Old Testament where, in each
case, their children were included in the special relationship
they made with God (Genesis 9:8, 17:7, Exodus 20:1–6).

Paul's attitude to the day-to-day life of children shows a
development from the Old Testament, too. Where children's
duties are specifically stated (Ephesians 6:1, Colossians 3:20),
they stand in conjunction with the duties of adults toward
them. Children are to respect, but parents (no longer just
fathers) are to avoid making them angry. Children are to

43

obey, but parents are not to irritate or discourage. Nurture has become a two-way process.

All these hints and contrasts, the New Testament transforming the Old, suggest that it was Jesus' intention that children should contribute as much to adults as adults to children. They may respond to God in different ways, but they can stand side by side as they approach him. That is why model four is a helpful base from which to begin thinking about what a Sunday School is for.

## The importance of knowing your aims

Practically every Sunday School has good intentions — but that is not the same as having worthwhile aims! In the weekly hurly-burly of making visual aids, breaking up scuffles, planning next week and scraping chewing gum off chairs, it is easy for leaders to avoid thinking together about their aims for years on end. Is this important? Well, God is very gracious and allows many good things to happen by accident — but if you do not know what your aims are, how do you know whether or not you have a successful Sunday School?

It is possible to imagine two leaders working side by side. One believes that her task is to provide a programme for the children of adults who are part of the church congregation. The other has decided that his task is to attract children from all over the area, many of whom have no other connection with the church at all. They have never discussed what the aims of the church's children's work are. One of them has been quietly thrilled for many months about the way the children of Christian parents have been growing up in Jesus. The other has been nursing a sense of failure that no children whose parents do not attend the church have stayed for any length of time. Neither of them has a wrong vision of what Sunday Schools can do. They just haven't decided which of two valid aims is right for the church at that time. It may be that they never get to think about whether what they are achieving is worth the effort until the man announces that he wants to leave! How much more satisfactory it is if leaders can sit down together occasionally to discuss their hopes for the future!

## Eighteen good reasons for running a Sunday School

1   To find opportunities for children to be an active part of the whole church fellowship.
2   To give parents the support they need to bring their children up in the Christian faith.
3   To make initial links with families who have no other church connection.
4   To produce the future adult generation of the church.
5   To keep the children of the adult congregation occupied while their parents worship.
6   To teach, pastor and worship with the children of the adult congregation.
7   To teach children Bible stories.
8   To teach children how to understand and apply the Bible.
9   To teach children to worship God.
10  To give children the opportunity to worship God.
11  To convert children to Christianity.
12  To allow children to grow up knowing Jesus.
13  To encourage children to develop good feelings about the church and Christianity.
14  To prepare children for membership of a denomination.
15  To give the children a really happy time.
16  To instil discipline and morality into children.
17  To help the children find fulfilment — spiritually, physically and emotionally.
18  To give leaders an opportunity to serve God and develop in their Christian lives.

## How do you decide what your aims are?

I have a pretty shrewd idea that, as you read through those aims, there were none you could positively say were bad things to do, but some seemed to you very much more important than others. That's natural — if you didn't think something similar, you weren't concentrating, so go back and read them again!

Making up your own mind is easy. It is much more difficult to come to a joint opinion with all the other leaders, but it is worth thrashing it through. There are several things to take into account as you decide. What is the tradition of your church and for what could you find backing from the leadership? What can you provide staff for? What do the children you currently have require? Are there children whom you want to reach, but do not at the moment? What Christian experience are the children getting at home, at school or elsewhere? Are these aims seeking to help children to be Christians, or merely to know about Christianity? With all that to consider, it is unlikely that any two churches will come to the same conclusions!

## Turning aims into action

Once you have decided what you are about, it is vital to review the programme you have on offer, and see whether it is likely to fulfil those aims. Suppose you chose, 'To teach children how to understand and apply the Bible.' It should lead to a different sort of programme from, 'To teach children Bible stories.' It would mean that you cannot stop once the children can tell you who rescued the man that was mugged on the road between Jerusalem and Jericho. You would need to go on to involve the children in deciding what it means to them to copy the good Samaritan in their day-to-day lives. It might involve discussion, improvising and acting out modern-day examples, or drawing pictures in which they themselves are behaving like the Samaritan at school or on the street. The methods would vary, but the point of them is the same — to give children the tools and skills they need to apply the Bible's teaching to their own actions and make plans for change.

As another example, if you picked out, 'To help children find fulfilment — spiritually, physically and emotionally', you need to ask yourself how you can achieve that. It may be that you find it is impossible to do so within the confines of

Sunday worship, where time and space are at a premium. In some churches, the desire to meet that aim has led to starting a midweek meeting. At that time, they provide the games and exercise which children need for their physical development and occasions to talk and develop relationships so as to respond to their emotional needs. Of course, it is quite possible to do these things on a Sunday too — but it often means restructuring the programme to make space for them. It is easy to say that you are concerned for the whole child, not just his soul — more difficult to turn that concern into action.

## How do you know it's working?

Most leaders have a sense of whether their Sunday School is going well or not, but a general feeling of well-being (or the opposite) is not likely to prompt the visionary changes through which God's work grows. Aims are, by definition, so wide-ranging that it can be difficult to know whether or not they have been achieved. This means that a series of objectives is also needed so that you can set specific targets — so specific that at the end of, say, a year, you can look at them and know instantly whether or not you have fulfilled them.

Let me give an example. If the aim of your Sunday School is, 'To make initial links with families who have no other church connection', you will never fully succeed. Excuse my lack of faith but, with thousands of unchurched families in the vicinity, to attract a child from every single one of them into the group is not possible. However, it is possible to set yourself a specific objective in January which states, 'We would like to have four new children settled into the group as a result of encouraging members to bring friends.' The following December, you will know whether or not you have fulfilled your objective. Of course, the number could be one or a dozen — but it will leave you neither guilty nor smug at the end of the year, when you evaluate your achievements. If you have not fulfilled your objective, you will need to ask yourself whether the programme you run is one in which children with no Bible knowledge or experience of Christianity can feel comfortable. What makes it so different from a programme solely for Christian children?

Would another example help? 'To teach children to worship God' is a very general aim. A specific objective which you could assess at the end of the year is, 'To progress to the stage at which most children are comfortable to read aloud prayers which they have written.' It is only a tiny part of learning to worship God, which is a lifetime's work, but it is one step along the way which is achievable in twelve months.

Although the aims of the children's work in a church will change quite slowly as years go by, the objectives can be thought out anew at the beginning of each year. Developing this as a regular practice ensures that you do not go on running activities in a particular way long after the reason for doing so has passed. It means that you can gear a programme to the children in your care now, not try to force the children through a programme that was ideal for a very different group ten years ago. The process looks like this:

## Aims and names

For the last four chapters, I have been referring to the children's work of a church as Sunday School. I'm going to continue because, if I use that name, everyone knows what I'm talking about. However, it is becoming increasingly obvious that the kinds of activity that I have been asking you to consider are not remotely like school, and the scope of them does not make it inevitable that they happen on a Sunday.

In fact, the more I think about it, the more daft the name seems to be! I keep thinking of a ten-year-old boy in the playground on a Monday morning being asked by his friends what he did yesterday. I can imagine the words 'Sunday School' sounding so boring and authoritarian that he would mutter them under his breath or talk instead about what he watched on television. (Goodness knows what he would do if the group was called 'Little Saints' or 'Sunshine Corner' or something really icky!) He would be in a far better position to give a positive witness to following Christ if he could use a name that he takes pride in.

The names used in the Scripture Union scheme — Adventurers, Lazer, etc. — all speak of excitement. There are others too — Explorers, Pathfinders, Discoverers, Lighthouse, The Factory. Acronyms are possible — the JAM club sounds tasty, and leaves open the possibility of explaining that it stands for 'Jesus And Me'. While we are jettisoning the name 'Sunday School', can we lose all the titles that go with it too? We honestly don't need teachers — we need leaders! We certainly don't need classes — we need groups! They express far more accurately the values of the 'learning together' model than academic words. Having said that, it is no good just changing all the names and leaving the features of the school room behind. No matter what thrilling name you give to a Scripture Exam, the thought of it still sends a shudder down a thousand spines.

As in everything else, try to see through a child's eyes, and look for ways of describing all your activities in terms of adults and children seeking to love and serve God side by side.

## Things to do

**1** Go through the list of eighteen reasons for running a Sunday school. Put a 0 against any that you would discount for your own church. Put a 1 against any that you broadly agree with and a 2 against those you think are particularly important. Show your list to other leaders who work with children of any age in your church and find out where they agree and disagree. Try to discuss your reasoning and come to a common mind.

**2** Decide whether you think your Sunday School, given the current staffing and resources, should aim to reach children whose parents are in the adult congregation on a Sunday, or those children and their immediate friends, or all the children of the area, including those who have no connection at all with a church.

Having decided, make a list of things the group ideally should do to serve that category of child, as distinct from the other categories, Circle the ones that you already do. Looking through the others, put a cross by those which are simply impossible and a tick by those which could be achieved with a concerted effort.

**3** Go through the items which have a figure 2 or a tick and pray that God will enable you to fulfil them. Thank God for the activities you circled and the aims you think you meet satisfactorily. Then, in front of God, make a conscious decision not to feel guilty about the other children and activities which are beyond your scope.

# 5
## Taking the pain out of learning

Did I tell you that I used to teach in a primary school? They were the happiest few years of my life! I still see most of my first class quite regularly. Susan was nine when she moved into the area and joined my class, but her reading age was only five. For the first few weeks I was virtually running a separate class just for her. She couldn't write a story, she couldn't record a science experiment, and she couldn't follow written instructions for a project. You see the size of her problem — which became mine! There was one thing Sue could do really well. She could recite her multiplication tables with great speed and complete accuracy.

'One times five equals five, two times five equals ten, three times five equals fifteen. . . .'

'Well done, Susan. So if I get out three plates and put five fish fingers on each of them, how many have I got altogether?'

'. . . .?'

'What are three times five?'

'Fifteen.'

'So if I have three lots of five fish fingers, how many are there altogether?'

Absolute silence!

I think I know what was wrong. My guess is that Sue's previous teacher had despaired of her ever learning anything. At the end of her tether, she had decided to stuff Sue's memory with tables, so that at least she had something to show for her term's work. Sue dutifully learned the words, but her teacher never bothered to let her find out how to use them or what they were for. It was just useless information.

So I set to work! Susan spent hours and hours making little piles of objects and counting up the totals. Three sets of five cotton reels, three packs of five *Mars* bars, three hands with five fingers on them, and so on. I can still remember her bewildered excitement as she discovered that every time she made that combination, no matter what the objects were, the result was magically and mysteriously the same. It astonished her! She thought it was wonderful! She became addicted and would plead to be allowed to get the maths equipment out — the only multiplication junkie I have ever known!

What's all this got to do with church?

Well, it reminds me of a danger to which Sunday Schools lay themselves open. There is a risk that we will content ourselves with telling children scores of Bible stories, glad when they can reproduce the facts, but never stopping to show children how to make use of the information they have gained. That is not really as worthless as learning tables by rote without knowing their purpose — God is very gracious and uses all kinds of experiences — but the two have some things in common. How very much more valuable it would be if children not only knew the content of the Bible, but were able to understand it and apply it to their lives.

Let me suggest an experiment! The story of Noah's ark is one that substantial numbers of children know well. Ask a group of them what they think the story means and what it teaches us about God. Comments by Jesus and Peter in the New Testament show us that it is about God's offer to save those who have faith in him from the consequences of sin. But I'd stake my last fruit gum that children will tell you it's something to do with animals!

*Learning by discovery.*

## Learning by discovery . . . learning by what?

What we long for is a generation of children who not only *know* Christianity, but also *do* Christianity. We need children not only to hear the Bible, but also to comprehend it. We need them not just to take the Bible in, but to work out what response it requires of them too. The first step towards achieving this is to allow children to take an active role in the Sunday School instead of sitting back and letting Sunday School happen to them.

One of the terms that has become jargon in schools is 'learning by discovery'. It means that instead of children being given information which they must learn (like being told how a tadpole grows from spawn and turns into a frog), they are given everything they need so that, under supervision, they can discover this information for themselves (they could be given some frogspawn, which they would observe, draw, discuss and write about over a long period as it develops). The point of it is that, having 'lived through' the lesson, rather than just heard about it, children learn it much deeper, better and more memorably. A by-product is that it is a lot more interesting to do, and life is more pleasant in every conceivable way when children are enjoying what they learn! It is learning by discovery which has led to the huge improvement in primary schools in the last generation. And there is absolutely no reason why Sunday Schools should not benefit from it as well!

Suppose children did not just hear Bible stories read to them, but could get inside them and live them out in their imaginations. What a difference it would make to the way they remembered them and understood the experiences of the characters! This can be done in a great variety of ways — by acting out the events, by discussing what the feelings of the real-life participants were, by all kinds of art and craft work, by looking at imaginative visual aids, by listening to the stories told in a way which zaps along with action and realistic detail, by attempting puzzles which are so much fun that children are longing to grab a Bible and find out the answer. All these methods count as learning by discovery, because in them children are taking responsibility for finding out important things for themselves.

## The problem of the culture gap

In the same way that children need to know the alphabet before they can use a dictionary, so it is impossible for children to make sense of God's word without help in making the leap between their culture and the Bible's. Because, as adults, we have become so familiar with the world of the Bible, we forget what a sizable problem it is for children to pitch their imaginations to a time almost irretrievably distant in the past and a country they have probably never seen, thousands of kilometres away, as different from their own as it is possible to be.

Frankly, it's hard enough for adults to think themselves back into first century middle eastern culture, rather than dragging the stories forward into our culture. To prove the point, test yourself! Imagine yourself to be beside the manger a few hours after the birth of Jesus — try to picture it in as much detail as possible. I'll give you a few moments, then I'll ask some questions. . . . OK?

What were the walls of the stable made of? If you pictured wood or brick or some kind of wattle and daub, you're a bit wide of the mark. Most archaeologists now think that any outhouse substantial enough to keep cattle in would have been a cave, not a building. And what did you imagine that Jesus was lying in? I guess there is a good chance that most people thought of a wooden cradle-like affair, whereas animals would have fed from a stone trough. And finally, what on earth were swaddling clothes? Congratulate yourself if you saw them as ripped-up strips of cloth made of wool, camel hair or anything else that had finished its useful life for someone else. If you saw some kind of white, polyester-and-cotton job, don't worry, you weren't alone! Now be honest! Was the stable you imagined more like a dark, smelly Israelite shelter, or a rustic Victorian barn preserved by the National Trust somewhere in Dorset?

Now add to that the confusion of a child who, educationalists inform us, develops no sense of place, apart from that which he has seen, until he is about ten, and no sense of historical progression until he is twelve or thirteen. It becomes apparent that to rush into Bible teaching without allowing children first to cross the bridge between their culture and Hebrew culture is unwise.

Put yourself in the position of a seven-year-old hearing the story of Hannah dedicating Samuel to God's service in the Temple by giving him to Eli as soon as he was weaned (1 Samuel 1:24–28). Without having had an introduction to the customs of the time, would you see Hannah's actions as godly or cruel? The latter, I suspect, for you would imagine yourself watching your mother depart, as you tearfully struggled to escape the grip of a strange old man. Even a fourteen-year-old with a thorough sex education would picture Samuel as a baby, not realizing that he wouldn't have been weaned until he was nearly four.

Every Bible passage brings its own problems. Several of the Gospel narratives are about people with a distressing skin disease, leprosy. It is easy for children to identify with being ill — they have all experienced it, although not often in such a disfiguring or harrowing way. But to understand the significance of Jesus' attitude to those who had leprosy, they need to be aware of the appalling social stigma that went with the disease — sufferers being compelled to live by themselves in isolated places so as not to spread the infection, surviving by begging from travellers and being treated with contempt. Knowing this, Jesus' actions in touching and healing them are seen not only as miraculous, but as radically compassionate. These are stories that children and adults alike need not just to marvel at, but to feel with their emotions.

## Building bridges

Here are some ways of helping children find their way from their own experience and knowledge back into a distant, but no less real, culture. They are all things which can be done before a Bible story is told or Christian truths are explored.

### Dressing up

Start young! There is a great deal that children can learn simply by trying out the clothes that their counterparts in New Testament times would have worn. Provide a dressing up box and leave children to be imaginative. A glance at a Bible encyclopaedia will show you what to include, and almost everything that Bible children would have worn can be adapted from worn-out materials that happen to be around the home. Men's headsquares can have had an active life as tea-towels, and net curtains can be put into retirement as women's veils. You will also need tunics, which were long pieces of material folded in the middle and sewn up the sides, leaving openings for arms and legs (a sheet will make two!). Cloaks are easy to fabricate and belts have not changed much in two thousand years. As you talk with children about what they are doing, point out that Bible characters did not dress in this way because it was quaint! They might have died from the heat of the noon sun without head-coverings, and the belt was functional because, when there was hard

work to be done, they could gather all the loose material of their tunics and tuck it out of the way.

Do not underestimate the age at which dressing-up will appeal. Ten- and eleven-year-old children studying, say, the ten commandments will enjoy making phylacteries out of matchboxes and card to demonstrate how the Jews took the instructions in Deuteronomy 6:6–8 literally. To borrow a prayer-shawl or skull-cap from a Jewish family which still makes active use of them would be even more revealing.

## Role-play

The next step on from dressing up is role-play, a teaching method which can go on being used all through the teenage years and among adults. It involves children putting themselves in the position of characters in the Bible and acting or moving or speaking as if they were those people. They will need quite strong direction as to what to imagine themselves doing, but within those limits they should be free to improvise movements or words and express emotions.

It is easiest to show how this works with an example. You might be investigating the story already mentioned, in which Jesus healed a group of men with leprosy (Luke 17:11–19).

In the story, ten diseased men pleaded from a distance for Jesus to take pity on them. As they walked away they found themselves healed, but in only one of them did it lead to faith in Jesus. He returned to thank Jesus and praise God.

You might start by describing to the children what effect leprosy had (and still has) on the body. Pictures and descriptions would help. Then ask the children to walk around the room for a minute, imagining they have the disease. How would they move? What impact would the combination of numbness and pain have on the way they walk, balance and turn? Children take some time to learn how to take this seriously. If they behave foolishly or make a noise, stop the activity and ask them to stand still. Point out that a technique of good acting is being realistic and trying your hardest not to overact. Stress that the people who are best at miming succeed in doing it without any noise at all. Will they be able to act well by being silent and realistic? Then ask them to try again.

Next, ask them to pretend they are in a market in first century Israel. They must decide what they are going to act out — selling vegetables, or buying material — all in mime. One of them will role-play the part of a man or woman with leprosy. When the market is at its busiest, he or she will walk through it. How will the people in the market-place react? When you have tried it out, ask the child who was playing the person with leprosy how it felt to be rejected and backed away from in this way. Can they put it into words? Ask those playing customers and salesmen what feelings they had towards the 'outcast' who had disturbed their day.

Having allowed the children to 'feel', as well as hear, what leprosy involved, ask them to imagine again that they have the illness. This time, as they walk round the room, they suddenly discover that they are not diseased any more. What do they notice first? That they can manipulate their fingers? That their legs move more freely? What difference will it make to the way they move? Will they be excited, delighted, elated? How would they show that? When they have tried it out, ask some of them again to put into words the differences

and their emotions. Always finish by thanking and congratu-
lating the children.

After that 'bridge-building' role-play, you can go on to tell
the Bible story in confidence that the children understand
more of it 'from the inside'.

## Sharing experience

Another way to bridge the gap is to concentrate on things
which are shared by the cultures, rather than different. Basic
emotions such as love, anger, fear or sadness have not
changed, because they are part of human nature. By high-
lighting things in the children's current experience it is possible to 'signpost' in advance features of a Bible story that you
particularly want them to learn. This should be done by
discussion, with the children talking about their lives, not the
leader telling children what he thinks their lives are like
(which in the case of seven-year-olds would probably be
wrong, and in the case of eleven-year-olds would probably
be resented). You will find more help about how to lead a
discussion later in the book.

A session which looks at the story of Joseph's coat can
uncover valuable truths about how God wants us to treat
other members of our families. You could begin with the
question, 'What issues start arguments in your families?'
Make a list with a felt marker on the back of a neatly-cut
piece of wallpaper, or on an overhead projector. As children
suggest answers from their own experience — which television channel to watch, whether it is compulsory to eat
everything put on your dinner plate, whether older brothers
and sisters should get more pocket money than younger ones,
and so on — explain that although the details have changed,
the feelings are very much the same as they would have been
in Bible families. Then go on to look at the Bible account
(Genesis 37), where identical problems of jealousy, favouritism, suspicion that others are getting a better deal, showing
off and laziness are all evident.

Starting in this way, it will not be hard for the children to
imagine the vibrations that were shaking Joseph's family. It
will also move the centre of interest away from the attention-

grabbing 'technicolour dreamcoat', which is really incidental to the story, and replace it with serious thinking about the important warnings of the passage.

## Fact-finding

Older children can put themselves in a better position to understand the Bible by researching the subject in the numerous encyclopaedias and Bible dictionaries that now exist, many written specifically for their age group. They could then discover, for instance, the real significance of Joseph's clothes. They would find out that 'multi-coloured coat' is actually a poor translation of a Hebrew phrase which should read 'coat with long sleeves'. The reason that Jacob gave it to Joseph was to make it impossible for him to do any more manual work — the sleeves would have got in the way. No wonder the brothers resented this blatant sign of favouritism, for it meant extra work for them. Oh of course — now it all makes sense!

## Games and simulations

Another way of helping children to uncover the concepts that the Bible teaches us is to recreate those concepts 'live' in games and activities which simulate them. To a young child, the idea that to follow Jesus means to emulate the good things he did is not a simple one. At that age, children think only in literal terms, so the connection between the ideas is not evident. However, playing 'Follow the leader', in which success means copying precisely the actions of a leader, makes the connection much more obvious. And it also makes the discovery an enjoyable and positive one.

Older children can learn from play as well. The parable of the tower builder in Luke 14:28–30 cries out to be played as a game. Allocate to each of several teams a pile of toy building bricks. They have a given time limit in which to run relay-style and collect bricks one at a time. When they have gathered what they judge to be the optimum number, they stop collecting and start to build a tower. If they have spent too little time picking up bricks, their tower will not reach its potential height, and there will be time going to waste at the end. If they have gathered bricks for too long, they will run out of time in which to add them to the tower. The whole point of the parable is lived out in real experience right there on the spot. The leader can go on to talk about how this shows us the importance of preparing seriously to give all it takes to be Jesus' disciple before we start out — which is precisely how Jesus explained his tale (Luke 14:33). The children have not just heard the parable though — they've done it.

## Choosing the correct method

With so many 'bridge-building activities' to choose from it may be difficult to know which is best. There are certain questions to consider which will help you decide. Firstly, read the Bible passage carefully and ask yourself what historical or cultural differences exist in the story which children will need to come to terms with before they can get to the real point that it is making. Secondly, ask yourself what is the prominent feature of the story that you want to 'signpost' by drawing on the children's present-day experience of comparable situations. Thirdly, bear in mind the ages of the children you have and search for a method by which that age-group could creatively discover the information for themselves, rather than sit and listen to it explained. And fourthly, make up your mind to go for it, praying that the Holy Spirit will reveal worthwhile things to the children.

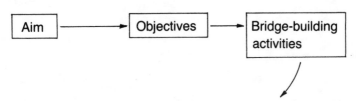

*The aim, objectives and programme now look like this.*

There are many books and schemes on the market which help you run a Sunday School. Not all of them deal properly with the problem of crossing the culture gap, and it is wise to examine how helpful a scheme is in this area before you choose it. Personally, I recommend Scripture Union's *Learning Together* scheme, which treats as a priority the need for children to understand the Bible thoroughly. But then I would, wouldn't I!

## Things to do

**1**   Read Luke 10:30–35. What are the differences between your culture and first century Jewish culture which might prevent the children realizing how shocking it is that a Samaritan should give the help which a priest and a Levite refused to give? If you are not sure, look up 'Samaritan' in a Bible dictionary.

**2**   How could you help the children discover what it felt like to be a Samaritan surrounded by Jews? Have you chosen a more effective way than simply telling them?

**3**   What do you think is the point of the parable? Compare your answer with Jesus' comments in Luke 10:29, 36–37. The children in your Sunday School will never meet a Samaritan — about which contemporary groups of people would you want them to change their opinion if they were to respond to Jesus' challenge to 'go and do the same'? How can you help them reach the conclusion that God wants us all to change our opinions in this way, without giving an authoritarian lecture?

# 6
## Putting the skin on Jesus

Dai Lewis, Scripture Union's highly-respected evangelist for Kent, tells a story about friends of his who were holidaying as a family in a remote part of Wales. Facing the dubious pleasures of managing without electricity or water on tap, the young daughter of the family was hesitant about going into the dark corners of the cottage alone. At bedtime, she grasped her mother tightly with one hand, a candle with the other, and made her way up the stairs. As she reached the bedroom and sat down among the shadows, the candle tipped over and went out. She didn't scream or panic, but she held on to her mother more urgently than ever.

'Be brave!' her mother said reassuringly. 'I'm going to go back downstairs and get the matches. But there is no need for you to be frightened, because even though I shall be gone for a couple of minutes, Jesus will be here with you.'

'Oh Mummy!' whispered the girl. 'Couldn't you stay here and we'll send Jesus for the matches?'

Later on, someone asked her what had led her to say this. She explained that she wanted her mother near as well as Jesus because her mother 'has skin on her'. I learnt a great deal from that comment, and became convinced that my task in helping children to explore the content of the Bible is to 'put skin on Jesus'. I want him to become a real figure to children, alongside all the other genuine, historical characters of the Bible, not just a half-real, half-fairy-tale figure like Hercules or St George.

Having prepared themselves with bridge-building activities, described in the last chapter, children will be well equipped to accept the reality of a Bible story when they hear it told. The next stage in each session's programme of learning and worship is to allow them to find out what the Bible has to say. But that need not merely mean listening to a passage being read aloud — there are many vivid and exciting ways of making the Bible come to life.

## Storytelling

There is only one way to get better at telling Bible stories — that is to try it out. Children will show you when you are getting it wrong by fidgeting, looking blank or misbehaving. Adults, if you have asked them to watch and be honest, will show you when you are getting it right and may be able to give you helpful comments. Here are some thoughts to start with.

### Preparation

Read the Bible story carefully in a modern translation, even if you know it well. Decide what God wants us to learn from the story — an example to copy, a warning to take seriously — and think about how that truth applies to children. Do not, however, shut yourself to the possibility that God will teach the children truths that you never dreamed would emerge from that passage.

Then choose from which point of view you will tell the story. You could tell it in the third person: 'Benjamin was always game for an adventure. He had already fallen into the stream that tumbled down the hill into Lake Tiberias. He wasn't in the slightest bothered about getting his bottom wet — he was more concerned to make sure he didn't splash the five bread rolls and pair of smoked fish that his mother had given him for lunch.'

Alternatively, you could tell it in the first person: 'I had never seen so many people in one place — I heard someone guess there were five thousand, and I should think they were right! I came because I'd heard that he performed miracles — Jesus that is. You should have heard what he said! Fascinating things! I could have listened all night. In fact, I was so interested that it wasn't until way past my usual mealtime that I realized how hungry I was. I was just unpacking the food I had brought with me, when. . . .'

Prepare the story really thoroughly. It needs a framework — an *introduction* with something interesting to grab attention in the first couple of sentences (such as the child's eye-view in the two examples above), *action* described with lots of vivid words, direct speech and feeling, a *climax* where the main point of the story is made absolutely clear, and a *conclusion* to tie up the ends.

You should definitely try to get to the point where you can *tell* the story, rather than read it, since that is about three times more effective. It may be that the first few times you present a story to children, you need it written out in full to give you confidence. Fair enough. . . . but the sooner you can let go of your script and rely instead on a series of 'headlines' or notes to jog your memory, the better the result will be.

Help yourself to keep the children's interest by making visual aids and pictures. As a rough guide, you need one for every minute that the story lasts. Make sure that they are big enough for the children to see easily. A trick-of-the-trade is to write your 'headlines' on the back of the pictures so that, when you hold it in front of you, you can refer to the notes without it being obvious to the listeners.

### Delivery
Make sure that the children are comfortable. Try having them sit on a rug if they are young, or in a semi-circle on chairs if they are older. You should be able to see the eyes

suspicious    angry    surprised

worried    puzzled    proud    sad.

of each child, so the ideal position is to have their heads on a level somewhere between your waist and your chest.

Relax and tell your story. Look at the children and keep eye contact with them (that's why you need to avoid reading word for word). You will have less discipline problems if you can look fidgety children in the eye!

Vary your facial expression to show the feelings of the characters. You are a visual aid, just as much as your pictures. You can also use your hands to indicate size or shape and to make gestures. By varying the pitch, tone and speed of your voice, you can make the story more dramatic as well.

If you think you are boring the children, slow down! I know that sounds ridiculous, but if you say, 'And you'll never guess what happened next . . . !' followed by a tantalizing pause, you may find that you have everyone's attention.

### Some examples
I had a shot at preparing to tell a Bible story. The one I chose is given in Genesis 32 and 33. This is a bit of an indulgence since it is my favourite story in the entire Bible. It is concerned with the need to seek reconciliation rather than revenge, so the story needs to be told in a way which

encourages children to realize that God expects us to copy these virtues in our own family lives.

I started thinking about the older end of the seven to eleven age-range. In the introduction to the story I needed to recap what had already happened to Jacob in case any children had not heard the first part of the story. I also wanted to create a certain amount of tension, to suggest a little of the bleak setting for the story and to picture Jacob as a real man with real feelings. I don't know whether I managed all that — you'll have to tell me:

'The hills of Gilead were steep and rocky, but Jacob walked across them like he was skipping through rich, green grass. He was going home! He had a beautiful family and flocks of sheep that stretched as far as the eye could see, and he was going home. He had made an agreement with his Uncle Laban that there would be peace in the family from now on, and he was going home. It was a great day and he knew that God was a part of it.

'There was one thing that bothered him. Twenty years ago he had left his brother Esau at home, seething with anger. Esau had made threats against Jacob's life which were so thinly disguised that no one would have been surprised to wake up one morning and find Jacob in his tent with an axe through his head. Twenty years was a long time! Jacob could imagine what two decades of anger would do to Esau — how mounting rage could drive a man mad for revenge. Of course, he was looking forward to seeing his mother and father again, but at the back of his mind was the fear he could not tell anyone about — that he might never reach them because of the killer brother in his shadow.'

After that I tried to keep the action zipping forward and to build up the suspense. To convey the tension when Jacob's messengers return from meeting Esau, these words were designed to build up the thrill of Genesis 32:6–7, without adding anything false to them:

'The message they brought sent an ice-cold shot of panic racing from the base of his spine to the hair on his neck. it was the message he had spent twenty years dreading he would hear. "We have seen your brother Esau. We did not even need to meet with him, because he has obviously heard from his spies that you are on your way. He is coming towards you at this moment. . . . and he has an army of four hundred men behind him." '

At the climax of the story, I wanted the children to realize that, although everything suggested that Esau should take revenge on Jacob, God's way demanded that they should forgive each other. I did this by deliberately leading children to expect a fight, making it all the more surprising when a reconciliation takes place. I slowed the pace of the story to a standstill before the dramatic surge of action:

'Jacob's final steps toward Esau were among the most painful he had ever taken. His eyes dodged between his feet, the horizon and the hem of Esau's tunic — he dared not catch his brother's eye to give away the fear that was trembling in him. Too soon he was close enough to Esau to hear the pace of his sandals on the gravelly sand. Almost without knowing what he was doing, he found himself bowing — five, six, seven times. It seemed the right thing to do, lower and lower until he was on his knees, quite still, head down to the ground. He froze there as he saw Esau approach — his feet, his cloak, the tip of his sword — and stop some ten paces away.

'There was a silence. A long silence! Jacob longed for the slightest sound — a bird, a cough, a locust maybe — to break the tension. But there was a deep silence, like the whole of eternity was focussed on this scene.

'Suddenly, there was a rush. Jacob saw Esau's feet flying towards him. He flung himself backwards on the ground and put his arms over his face to protect himself from the fatal blow that would slash down on to his neck. And then around his head crashed Esau's hairy arms with their sickeningly familiar feel and smell.

'Then, all of an instant, Jacob realized that this was not what he expected. The arms were not beating him, they were hugging him. The voice was not screaming of death, it was moaning sounds of love and happiness. And those eyes that Jacob visualized as full of hatred. . . . well, they were full of tears.

'And then Jacob was crying too. And hugging, and wrapping his arms around Esau. Then shouting out how wonderful it was to see his brother and, my word, practically dancing, and then crying all over again.'

The point had been made at this stage. There were a few details of the story left to cover, then it needed to move as fast as possible to its conclusion, which briefly summed up the major learning-point of of the story. You won't miss it, because it is alliterative to make it memorable:

'And there they stood in the morning sun, with their arms around each other. And there I think we should leave them! They've got a great deal of news to catch up on, after all. They ought to be allowed to talk in private. So we will turn away and think instead about God, who earnestly wanted there to be forgiveness, not fighting, in that family, and was infinitely kind to them, even though they did not deserve it.'

Next, I thought through the same story from the point of view of a younger child. It is obvious why the story above is less suitable for, say, a seven-year-old than for an eleven-year-old. There is complicated vocabulary, there are some fairly scary images and the involved sentences take too long to get to the point. Let me try the introduction again, this time for a young child:

'Have you ever been scared? I mean really scared! Jacob was. Twenty years ago he had done a very wrong thing. He had tricked his brother Esau and made him so angry that he had been forced to run away from home. He thought Esau was going to kill him. Imagine that — terrified of your own brother! Jacob had always dreaded the day when he would meet Esau again — and now that day was here. Jacob was so scared that he couldn't sleep at all — he spent the long night praying and praying and praying to God.'

This opening helps the child imagine himself into the story by beginning with familiar emotions — being scared and arguing with a brother. Most of the abstract words in the Bible account have gone. The background to the story has been given in a straighforward way and the sentences are fairly short. There is even an opportunity, after the first question, for children to join in.

If I were telling the story to very young children, say five and under, I would try to use a lot of enjoyable repetition. Possibly I would introduce a refrain for them to repeat at key points in the story, 'Jacob be careful, your brother is coming; Jacob be careful, your brother is near.' Pick up the story again later on:

'Everyone went quiet as they watched Jacob and Esau approach each other. Would there be a big argument? Would there be a terrible battle? Perhaps all the four hundred men who had come to protect Esau would sweep down and kill Jacob in front of them!

'These were the worst moments of Jacob's life. He took slow steps, bowing to Esau every few paces, seven times in all, to try to show him that he didn't want to fight. Suddenly, Esau rushed forward. He ran towards Jacob with his arms stretched out. He threw his arms around Jacob, but it was not to fight him, it was to give him the biggest hug he had ever had in his life. "Jacob it's good to see you," he said, but you could hardly hear it because he was so happy that he was crying.

' "I love you too, Esau," murmured Jacob, and all of a sudden he was crying as well. "Please forgive me." He hugged him even tighter. "I just want to be friends again, like when we were boys." '

It is appropriate to include just as much suspense for children of this age, but it must be shown more obviously. There is also more direct speech and straighforward action. The purpose of telling the story, that children should think about keeping peace with their families, is stated very obviously at the high point of the narrative. The conclusion needs to explain clearly why the story is important for Christians:

'Jacob gave Esau a lovely present. Esau said that he didn't want it really, because to be friends again with Jacob was the biggest present of all, but Jacob insisted and it made them both very happy. They didn't always live close to each other — in fact Esau moved his tents and lived quite a distance away. But for all the rest of their lives they never forgot what God had shown them — that it is much, much better to forgive other people in our families and live in peace with them, than to fight with them and try to get our own back.'

## Visual aids

'What's the use of a book,' thought Alice, 'without pictures or conversations?' I'm sure Lewis Carroll was not the first person to ask this question when he wrote it at the very beginning of *Alice in Wonderland*. A hundred years on, cinema, television and advertising have made the question even more pertinent. We live in a visual age and children have come to rely on visual images. (So have adults, but that's a problem for someone else's book!) If you are in any doubt that we need to use visual aids to communicate the Bible to children, make a mental list of all the television programmes you can think of that are made specifically for children, then make a list of all the radio programmes made specifically for children. Point made?

### The most valuable piece of equipment I know

If every single piece of technical equipment that is used in church was being taken away from me, I know which one I would cling to as they dragged me, screaming behind it, across the floor! I'd happily lose the microphones — I could always shout! I wouldn't mind losing the instruments — we could sing hymns unaccompanied! The machine which I would find it hardest to do without is an overhead projector. It is a box about the size of a biscuit tin out of which a light shines upwards. On it is a piece of transparent plastic and whatever you write or draw on the 'acetate' is reflected in a mirror above the box and projected on to a screen or wall about twenty times larger. It is quite an expensive item compared with, say, a blackboard, but has so many uses that I can recommend it unreservedly.

The simplest way to make an effective visual aid is to chose an illustration from a book of copyright free drawings (a Sunday School manual is ideal), put an acetate on top of it and trace it using a special overhead projector pen. This needs to be done in advance, so that when you are telling the story all you need to do is place the acetate on the

projector and switch the bulb on. The picture will then be large enough for up to a hundred children to see. One leader can tell the story, so it is not wastefully duplicated by half a dozen leaders, each with a little group and a handful of tiny pictures. It is so easy it ought to be a crime!

As you use it more, you will discover how to make the illustrations varied and even more interesting by using silhouettes, different colours, combinations of words and pictures, and images built up one piece at a time by laying acetates on top of each other. The possibilities are endless and it is all as simple as using tracing paper.

**Doing-it-yourself**
Never, never underestimate your own abilities! I failed my art O-level so spectacularly that I was not even given a grade, but I would never go into a Sunday school without visual aids. I use every method of cheating that I can think of! I rip pictures out of children's Bible story books, cut round figures in the positions I want them — sitting, standing, laughing, crying — and attach them to a background in various combinations, using *Blu-Tack*. I have built up a huge

stock of them now — yesterday's Moses will be tomorrow's Abraham.

I trace around figures which happen to be in the position I want them and display them as silhouettes. The trick is to know which colours show up well against each other — diplay black on white or yellow, red on green, blue on orange.

I make glove puppets by pushing my forefinger through a paper bag and putting a matchbox on it. Even I am able to cut a circular face out of brown paper, add eyes, nose and a mouth and paste it on the matchbox to produce a Middle Eastern face.

I draw pin-men and blob women as I tell the story so that the children can see the illustrations created before their very eyes. What they don't see is that I have already drawn the shape in very faint pencil before I arrive. I have got the positions right by trial and error, and simply draw over the lines with a felt marker.

I make little models of people by twisting pipe cleaners together and tying pieces of material around them. If I need a king and his soldiers I eat a *Kit-Kat* and mould the silver paper into a crown or a sword. An extra advantage of models like this is that they can be pushed into different shapes — kneeling, bowing, shrugging — as the story progresses.

The biggest cheat of all is sometimes the one that is of most value to the children. I ask them to make a frieze or a model of a cartoon strip, giving them clear instructions as to what I need. Then I use their pictures as I tell the story, making positive remarks all the time about how much help they have given me.

None of these methods of making visual aids have ever required the slightest artistic talent on my part whatever — which is just as well! All I have ever needed is the cheek to get away with it!

## Word and captions
It is easy to forget that simply writing words on sheets of paper is an effective visual aid for children who can read. To display large cards, one after another, reading 'Jacob and

his family', 'Jacob is fearful', 'Jacob — will he fight?' 'Jacob is forgiven' marks out the development of the story.

You will probably have passed thousands of road signs without ever having questioned why they are written mainly with lower case letters, not block capitals. It is because this makes them easier to read, which is important at speed! Likewise, all lettering in captions, displays or visual aids for children should use capitals only at the beginning of names or sentences. This is what children experience at school. Once again, experiment is the best teacher!

## Using the Bible with children

True or false? 'The Bible was not written for children, so there is little point in expecting them to read it.'

# Lettering

Use upper and lower case

NOT CAPITALS *or joined up*

Neither too thin        nor small

Draw lines if it helps

Try it in pencil first *so you don't get squeezed at the end*

Well, the first part is true, but I don't think it leads automatically to the second part. The Bible, after all, was not written for twentieth century adults either, but that doesn't mean that it is not applicable to them. It does mean, though, that it needs to be used wisely.

Jesus would have found out about the Old Testament by sitting in a straight row of Jewish boys at the feet of a rabbi, learning passages by rote. That approach simply is not appropriate for today's children, because the culture in which they live is so very different. So how should we find an appropriate equivalent?

Make sure that the children realize that what you tell them about God comes from the Bible, not your imagination. Have a Bible beside you at all times in the Sunday School. Refer to it — even show the children on which page you found the story that you are telling.

Encourage the children to own Bibles and bring them to Sunday School. Regularly, but not over-frequently (possibly once a week), ask children to look up a particular verse to show that something you want them to discover about God is contained there.

Avoid reading long passages if you are aware that this is boring children. The idea that the Bible is a boring book may take a long, long time to 'unlearn'.

Teach them how to look up a particular book, chapter and verse. This will be difficult if children own books of Bible stories, rather than complete Bibles. Explain the difference, without making a child who has a book of Bible stories in his or her hand feel inferior.

It is tremendously important to recommend a modern translation for two reasons. Firstly, new research and theologians' increased understanding of the way ancient languages work mean that modern translations are more reliable than those made in previous centuries. Secondly, it can only dismay children to struggle through vocabulary and syntax which they simply cannot understand. The *Good News Bible* was translated with the aim of being accessible to any child or adult with a reading age of nine years or older. While it would probably be fair to say that adults who want to take Bible study seriously also need a more scholarly translation with which to compare it, it's hard to make out a case for using any version other than the *Good News Bible* with children.

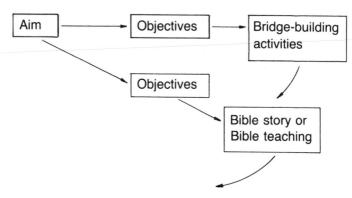

*The aim, objectives and programme now look like this.*

Obviously it is our desire that, at some stage, individual children will start to read the Bible of their own volition, not because someone persuades them that it would be a good idea. Give them every encouragement to develop the habit as a child. There are several Bible reading aids designed to cover the parts of the Bible which are most helpful for this age-group to read. They offer children the chance to discover a few verses every day, and use activities which children enjoy — puzzles, questionnaires, cartoons — to help them understand and apply their content.

Young boys and girls need support from an adult at home to help with difficult ideas and to urge perseverance. It may be worth talking to individual parents about what is available and explaining the value of Bible reading and the many other Christian books which are available to help children. This is part of the leaders' and parents' shared responsibility for the spiritual development of a child — of which parents will always need to bear the larger part. The Sunday School leader can be a real support in this area, but God is looking at parents to help the children he has given them grow up as his praying, serving, Bible-reading followers.

Children who do not find much enthusiasm for the idea from their parents find the discipline much harder — although by eleven they may be in a slightly better position to motivate themselves. They will be helped if they find regular interest in what they have learnt when they come to the Sunday School. If leaders can also share with the children what they have learnt from the Bible, so much the better.

It would be wrong if I failed to add that God did not make literacy a condition of becoming a Christian. He never turns away an adult who cannot read, and he never turns away a child for whom reading the Bible is an impossibly daunting task. Never give children, either consciously or unconsciously, the impression that they must be able to read the Bible to understand God or to please him. It's not only damaging, it's untrue! I reckon the chances are slim that Jesus' first followers — the fishermen, women, outcasts — were literate.

# Are you being completely biblical?

Before you answer that question, think carefully about whether you have told your children every story in the Bible. Even if you have (and that is unlikely, for some Bible stories are simply not suitable for children) you have only communicated about one third of the Bible. There are also letters, songs, proverbs, laws, prophecies — and that is just the beginning. Among these are valuable truths about God which children need to know.

There will be times when we need to tell children about Biblical truths as a series of points backed up with references from these other parts of the Bible. For example, it has become apparent in recent times that part of man's responsibility for God's world is to respect the Earth, oppose pollution and treat the whole of creation in a caring way. As hard as you look, you will not find a story in the Bible which teaches it — but repeated instructions in the Israelite Law, the prophets and Proverbs make it clear that God expects this of his people. Obviously, as children grow older, you will want them to think in an increasingly detailed way. With young children it might be appropriate to talk about a single verse (say Proverbs 12:10) and support it with a present-day story, true or fictional. This will not make the truth any less biblical! And it is, after all, precisely what Jesus did!

It becomes increasingly obvious that, in order to give children a thorough biblical education, we need to do more than tell well-loved stories over and over again. What is needed is a systematic syllabus which has been thought out months and even years ahead to give a comprehensive coverage of all the truths that we hope children will discover about God and the Christian life. It should cover not just one age-group, but the whole range of those being nurtured in our churches — toddler to adult. Several schemes on the market provide this — look carefully before you chose one, to see that it deals with the truths of the whole Bible, not just the ones which are easy to wrap up in a story.

The Bible wasn't originally written for children. Praise God that many people are devoted to making it accessible to them, both visually and linguistically. But if you find it completely easy to use the Bible with children, you can be reasonably sure that something is missing, and you ought to think again!

## Things to do

**1**  Record on a cassette, or write if you prefer, a story based on Jesus' parable in Matthew 13:44. When you have done so, give it to a friend and ask him or her to tell you which elements of it are good and how you could improve. To get you started, here are some questions which you need to consider:

(a)  What did Jesus want those who heard the parable to learn? If you are not sure, look at a Bible commentary.

(b)  How will you ensure that the children make the connection between the story and its meaning?

(c)  Will you tell the story in the first person (I) or in the third person (he)?

(d)  Will you set this timeless story in the first century or the twentieth century? In either case, what will the 'treasure' be when you describe it?

(e)  How will you grab the children's attention at the beginning?

(f)  How will you build up the suspense to make the children eager to know what the man has found in the field?

(g)  Would it be appropriate to use humour in the story — maybe when the man sells his every possession?

(h)  Can you think of an ending which makes it clear that the Kingdom of Heaven is even more valuable than the treasure?

**2**  There are many ways of presenting this visually. It is important to choose the best (not necessarily the easiest) for your Sunday School group. When you have decided which to use, prepare any visual aids you need and try it out. Possibilities are:

(a)  Pictures of some kind.
(b)  Silhouettes.
(c)  Puppets.
(d)  Models.
(e)  A real spade, treasure and bag of money to act with.
(f)  Miming as you tell the story with imaginary props.

# 7

## Your praise is sung by children

That is a quotation from Psalm 8, one of the psalms associated with David. He ought to know about children, he had enough of them! Jesus quoted it a thousand years later and made it sound even more forceful, 'You have trained children and babies to offer perfect praise.' He used the words in the Temple, having demanded that money changers and merchants leave it and restore it to its proper use as a place of prayer to God. The chief priests and religious teachers did not recognize this as a sign that Jesus was God's Messiah — but children did. They shouted, 'Praise to David's Son!' all round the Temple. It was this, rather than the overturning of the stalls, which really got the priests mad! But the children had it right — the adults once again lost their chance to learn from children. They were reacting to Jesus in the only way they knew. No one was telling them what words they should say, or that they should sit silently and listen (which they would have had to do in the synagogue). Jesus responded to their honesty. He still does!

It is possible to persuade yourself that, because the children shut their eyes and do not actually disrupt a leader's

80

long, formal prayer, they are communicating with God, or that because they stand and murmur the words of a famous hymn, they are worshipping him. God responds to their honest thoughts and actions. Sometimes that will mean the leader speaking to God on behalf of the children. But sometimes not!

## Helping children get through to God

When a leader positions himself in front of a group, shuts his eyes and starts to say a prayer, three things can happen. Either children listen, agree and repeat 'Amen' as a sign that they wish God to accept that prayer from them as well, or they retreat into their own private thoughts and imagination, or they communicate with each other in that informal sign language with which children are so inventive. I once heard of a group which managed to rearrange every single member on to a different seat while the leader had her eyes shut to pray — but I suspect that story is apocryphal! There are certain ways of making it more likely that the first of the three will take place.

## Leading prayers

Pray in the language that children use. 'Thou O Lord art highly to be praised because of thine exceeding holiness' is the language of another generation and there can't be many Sunday schools left which use words like that. However, there are also obstacles to the children understanding, 'Lord most high, you are so holy that you are worthy of our praise'. It uses an unfamiliar name for God (he sounds like a giant) and two complex religious words — holy and worthy (even 'praise' would need explanation for young children). The straightforward alternative is, 'Lord God, you are so great and so good that, when we think of you, we want to tell you how wonderful you are.' There is a temptation to go to the other extreme and use children's slang and playground talk. There is, of course, nothing wrong with children telling God that he is 'brill' or 'well good' if it is a genuine expression of how they feel about him — but if adults use words like

81

that on their behalf, children see through the trick a mile off!

Be brief! You can always have another time of prayer later in the programme, and God has the whole of eternity to wait!

Regularly and consistently offer prayers to which children will be able to see the answers. There will obviously be times when you need to pray such things as, 'Lord God, help us to obey you in all that we do', but it is difficult for children to judge whether or not God has responded to that prayer. If you believe that prayer actually changes the course of the world, then help children to learn that in practice. If they arrive in church concerned about a hijacked plane that they have seen on the news, pray for the release of the hostages. If the mother of one of them is going to give birth any day, pray for the safe arrival of the baby. This, of course, involves taking risks, for we know that God may respond to the prayer by effectively saying 'No' or 'Wait'. However, this is the way God works, and children need to find out about it at an early age, even if it is hard for leaders to explain. If children grow up thinking that they can only offer bland prayers, they will develop a bland faith.

Ask children to listen carefully and only say 'Amen' if they agree. It may mean that you only hear two 'Amens', but at least you know they are genuine. A lot of children think that 'Amen' means 'please'. In fact it means, 'Let it happen just as we have said', so to tell children that it means 'I agree' is only a whisker away from its literal translation.

It is good, from time to time, to use responsive prayers. These are prayers in which the children reply, 'We thank you, Lord', 'We are sorry, God', 'We love you, Lord' or some similar sentence, after each phrase spoken by the leader. The response needs to be brief enough for children to hold in their short-term memories. It is much more useful than asking children to repeat a prayer phrase by phrase, since they are almost certain to lose track of what the prayer was about before they reach the end.

## Giving children a voice

It is even more likely that children will be honest with God if they are using their own words. It is fair to say, though, that prayer is a skill which children need to learn — even if they eventually discover that praying is as natural as breathing. It is never too young to start, but don't expect a three year old instantly to pray like St Francis.

Introduce children to saying their own prayers by asking them to contribute one word. Encourage very young children to think of things for which they want to thank God. When each has suggested something, place them in order (so that they are comfortable that they know exactly when to speak) and invite them to say 'Thank you, God, for. . . .', one after another. Point out to them that, although God would listen even if they thought the prayer silently, the value of saying it aloud is that we can all join in. There are all kinds of variations, such as 'Please help my best friend. . . . (*name*).'

Older children can praise God in a similar way. They can be given cards which say, 'Lord God, when I think of you, I realize that you are. . . .', and be invited to write a word or phrase that completes the sentence and makes it true for them. Then they can read the cards in turn.

If children are really unhappy about saying words of praise aloud, they could write words which describe God on pieces of card in interesting colours and shapes. They might write 'powerful' or 'wise' or 'loving'. Then present a chart which is headed 'Lord God, we think you are ...'. Play a piece of inspiring music and suggest that children come one at a time to *Blu-Tack* their cards to the chart, as an act of worship.

Another step on the road to learning how to pray is to choose between various alternatives. After a session on using our gifts in God's service, children could be given a card from which they are to choose what they wish to say to God in response. The children opt for one of the endings, then read their prayers in turn. When you compose the alternative phrases, you need to remember that you must be prepared to accept any of them when the children come to pray.

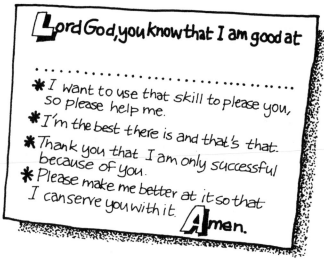

Lord God, you know that I am good at

. . . . . . . . . . . . . . . . . . . . . . . . . . . . . . . .

* I want to use that skill to please you, so please help me.
* I'm the best there is and that's that.
* Thank you that I am only successful because of you.
* Please make me better at it so that I can serve you with it. Amen.

This step-by-step method may lead you to the stage at which children can devise their own prayers, telling God of their own concerns. It will help their confidence in approaching God to be able to write down and read their prayers in the first instance. Some children find it easier to work in pairs. It is important not to give up at this stage if the prayers are given shyly or are not of a very high 'quality', because children will probably not feel completely at ease until they have done this many times.

It is often possible for children eventually to speak their prayers without writing them — just don't demand too much too soon! One way of helping practically is to sit children in a circle and give one of them a Bible or a card to hold. Explain that only the person holding it is allowed to speak, and when he or she has finished, the Bible will be passed to the next person. That person may say a prayer, or pass it on again if he or she prefers. In this way no one will ever be embarrassed by not knowing when to start (although you will want to explain that it is only needed to help *us* — God would happily listen to everyone at once).

In my experience, children who know God almost invariably want to speak to him. If they don't, it is because of lack of experience, encouragement or example. I was once helping to lead a Christian holiday for eight- to twelve-year-old children. The boys I had in my group were extremely enthusiastic when it came to prayer. If they had been as fervent about going to sleep at night as they were about talking to God, I would have come home a happier man! We were visited by the director of the missionary society which runs the holiday. He joined our group in the dormitory last thing at night when we were praying. The thanks and requests flowed on and on from the boys, until one of them nudged the man in the ribs and asked, 'What's wrong? You haven't prayed yet!' He did!

## By themselves

While helping children to pray, it must be our longing that one day they will do so unprompted, on their own. While it is true that the desire must come from the children themselves, the Sunday School leader can help by encouraging and giving a structure. Some good methods don't age! Donkeys' years ago my Sunday School leader gave me a teaspoon and suggested that I kept it by my bed. The TSP of 'teaspoon' stood for Thank you, Sorry and Please, and were to remind me of things I could say to God every night

*'My cup's what?'*

as I climbed into bed. I kept it there for a long time and developed a habit that I haven't yet managed to shake off! I don't think my mother ever realized what it was for! She once gave me a dose of penicillin with it and took it away, so I had to tiptoe down to the kitchen and retrieve it. Twenty years on, I visited some friends in Scotland and was requested to tuck their young daughter into bed as her 'treat'. I tiptoed into the bedroom, armed with *Winnie the Pooh* as a bedtime story, and guess what was on the table beside her bed. . . . !

## Music and singing

I think it was the fourth or fifth time that I sang, 'Running over, running over, my cup is full and running over', that I had the intelligence to ask myself, 'What are these cups and why are we running over them?' I wish that, as a five-year-old, I'd had the courage to ask the question aloud.

It goes to show how inappropriate are some of the things

we ask children to sing to God — inappropriate either because they are not true ('Since the Lord saved me, I'm as happy as can be'), or because the language they use is so metaphorical or poetic that its meaning is obscure ('Give me oil in my lamp, keep me burning').

It begs the question of why we sing at all. To allow the children to let off steam? Because they enjoy doing actions? To fill in time? To 'warm children up' for their teaching? These aren't good enough reasons in themselves. The only really good reason for singing is to let children tell God, and tell each other, what they think of him. Some of the other advantages can fall in place behind it, but that reason must dominate the songs that are selected and the position they occupy in the programme.

## Some things that go wrong

Lots of people say that older boys don't want to sing any more. It's such a common thing to say that I have written it myself elsewhere in the book. Well, I've stood beside my fourteen-year-old friends in changing room showers and at football matches and, if you think boys don't sing, you'll have to take it from me that you're wrong! So what makes a boy turn from Harpo Marx in the Sunday School to Bruce Springsteen in the nude and covered with mud?

It's not to do with creating the opportunity to sing, it's to do with creating the desire! The fact that public singing has become less of a part of daily life over the last twenty years means that children have cultural obstacles to overcome. If the life of the adult church and the desire to contact God prove that singing is worth the effort, then they will ignore the obstacles. But if the songs are too babyish, too complex, too boring, too difficult to sing, or go on for too long, then the barriers of embarrassment and, later, boys' breaking voices, will dominate.

That is why it is important to stress why we are singing from the earliest years. It is not a competition to show who can sing loudest or best. It is not to satisfy the musician. It is not even because singing is fun. It is simply to please God.

The easiest way for a child to learn a new song is to hear it. Don't teach it line by line (which is boring). Instead sing it, or ask the musician to play it with the melody line made really obvious, then have a go together. Try it again the following week.

Remember that children will never get further in worship than the adult congregation which they watch and emulate. If the adults clap, dance or raise their hands during songs, following the biblical tradition, then encourage the children to do so — and tell them why they are doing it! If the adults don't do actions, then there is not much point in teaching children to do so — subconsciously they will learn that enjoying worship is something that one grows out of. Having said that, if adults saw children praising God with sincerity and learnt to copy them, that would be something special!

## No music no worship?

Of course not! There are many ways of praising God and not all of them involve singing. If there is no musician on the Sunday School team (and you cannot persuade a friend to record a cassette tape accompaniment), or if the lack of response from children is too discouraging, investigate other methods.

Choose a psalm and use it to praise God. Split the group into two halves and ask one to read the odd numbered verses and the other to read the even ones. This is called 'reading antiphonally' and was a part of Jewish Temple worship. You can subsequently ask children, in pairs, to discuss which of the verses agrees most with what they think about God, and tell the others why.

You could also ask children to listen to a part (and it must be just a part) of a piece of Christian music, to help them think through the teaching they have had. Pitch this correctly so that five-year-olds are listening to simple songs, teenagers are listening to rock music, and every age between has something appropriate to their culture.

Equally, do not forget that children can use and be moved by silence in a valuable way, just as adults can. It helps, though, if the leader is very specific about what they should think about during the peaceful moments, and keeps it fairly short. Explain that sometimes God uses pauses like these to get a message through to people who are listening out for him, but tell the children not to expect a human voice, for it is more likely that God will communicate by putting good ideas inside their heads.

Look out, as well, for passages of the Bible which could be read to the praise of God. Examples are 1 Chronicles 29:10–13, the shouts of the angels in Revelation 4, or 2 Timothy 2:11–13, in which the leader can read the first half of each statement and the group respond with the second.

It is possible to devise chants, in which the leader reads lines to which children respond with a repeated assertion about God. Here is one:

When I see the Concorde flying,
*Life is lovely thanks to God,*
Sunset as the day is dying,
*Life is lovely thanks to God,*
Hear the roar of crowds at Wembley,
*Life is lovely thanks to God,*
Roller coasters turn me trembly,
*Life is lovely thanks to God,*
Trumpets sounding brash and tinny,
*Life is lovely thanks to God,*
Hot baths round me bare and skinny,
*Life is lovely thanks to God,*
Dewdrops hung on cobweb wisps,
*Life is lovely thanks to God,*
Taste of ready salted crisps,
*Life is lovely thanks to God,*
Smell of eggs and bacon cooking,
*Life is lovely thanks to God,*
Scratch an itch when no one's looking,
*Life is lovely thanks to God,*
Staying up till late at night,
*Life is lovely thanks to God,*
Then I shout with all my might,
*Life is lovely thanks to God.*

But chants need not be so complicated. In my Sunday School, the question 'What do we believe?' is answered with a bellow, 'Christ has died, Christ has risen, Christ will come again. Yeah!' On the final monosyllable, the whole group leaps alarmingly into the air. I didn't tell them to do this — it just seemed to happen! It is part of the 'wow factor' which I have come to see as a foundation of children's worship.

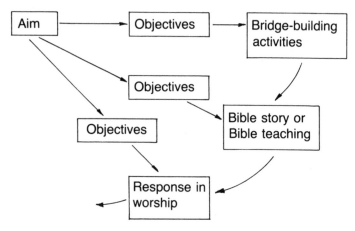

*The aim, objectives and programme now look like this.*

## Do you take this seriously?

My guess is that, if there are shortcomings in a Sunday School, they are more likely to be in the area of worship than anywhere else. Most leaders realize that the old-fashioned 'hymn, prayer, hymn, notices, hymn, split up for a story, goodbye' format did not help the children to grasp the reality of coming face-to-face with God in worship. But many don't know what to replace it with. This is even more striking when you see worship in its full sense — not just the praise given on a Sunday, but the value given to God overflowing from Sunday and flooding the rest of the week. Here are some suggestions to sum up:

If children are going to understand why they are worshipping, it probably needs to come as a response to what they have learnt, not before it. It also needs to be obviously relevant to the theme of each week's teaching.

Children and adults alike need to 'do' worship, not to have worship 'done to them'. That means giving children every encouragement to make their own decisions about what to pray from the earliest age. If worship is as important as we claim it is, then we need to give it a very high profile in the programme we devise. It is no good to relegate it to 'the opening song and the closing prayer'. It must take its place among the most exciting and involving things that happen in Sunday Schools.

## The offertory

And now, a quirky little final section about what is often a quirky little final activity. There are two schools of thought, one of which says that children ought to learn to give from their own pocket money, even if that means giving only a couple of pence. The other says that parents should give children money to put in the offertory as a model for them to copy later. My own concern is not for what children do, but for what they learn from doing it. I guess that a child who has learnt that it is part of serving and pleasing God to give a penny which he could have spent on sweets, has learnt something very valuable. My fear is that the child who simply passes on a more substantial amount doesn't give much thought as to why it has passed from a parent's pocket, *via* his hand, into a collecting bowl. The difference in financial terms is hardly worth speaking of — the difference in spiritual terms is huge.

It is good to take all the mystery out of giving. To say, 'The collection is being given to God', conjures up very odd images in the minds of young children, particularly if they see the treasurer bag it up and put it in his or her pocket! Most children, when asked what they think the money is spent on, say something like, 'To help poor people.' This may of course be true, but if it isn't (as will be the case in most churches) it is important to explain exactly what is done with the money. If it is used so that the church can continue to serve God and tell others about him, then explain it. To collect over a number of weeks and purchase a specific item for the church, or send a donation to a missionary or relief society, would also help children to understand that it is not just an admission fee.

One last word from hard-earned experience — make the offertory the first thing you do with children. That's got nothing at all to do with learning spiritual truths — it's got everything to do with the knees of your jeans after you've spent half the session crawling round the floor looking for lost coins!

## Things to do

**1**   Read Acts 3:1–10 and imagine that you are going to prepare a Sunday School session of worship and Bible learning based on that passage. These are your 'objectives' — the things you want the children to do:

To hear the story of how God healed a lame man when he met Peter and John.

To praise God, like the lame man did when he was healed.

To pray for anyone we know who is ill.

Think of several ways in which the children can do the second and third of those. Try to make them follow on naturally as a response to the Bible passage. Choose songs which are appropriate, not just fun to sing. Look for ways of praying and praising in which children are using their own thoughts, not just listening to someone else's. Include at least one which involves creative activity (a chart or picture) as well as or instead of words.

**2**   Having thought of several methods, choose the one or two items that are most appropriate to your own group and arrange them into an imaginary programme.

**3**   If it is possible, use them now as a basis for your own praise and prayer, part of your ongoing worship of God this week. Try not to think of this as a 'trial run' — mean your prayers in the way you hope the children will mean them.

# 8
# *Getting into action*

There is a fair amount of agreement that Sunday Schools should be places where children hear Bible stories and worship God. I want to suggest, though, that there are three things, not two, which should be urgent priorities. Children should hear Bible stories, worship God, and then work out what practical difference the truths they have discovered are going to make to their everyday lives.

It is a biblical principle. James writes, 'Whoever listens to the word but does not put it into practice is like a man who looks in a mirror and sees himself as he is. He takes a good look at himself, then goes away and at once forgets what he looks like. But whoever looks closely into the perfect law . . . and does not simply listen and then forget it, but puts it into practice — that person will be blessed by God in what he does' (James 1:23–25). There is, however, a tremendous danger here. If adults simply state, 'This is what you must do if you are a Christian . . .', there is every chance that children will be put under a pressure which they cannot cope with. If that danger is avoided, there is the equally unhelpful possibility that the instructions given from the perspective of

*Getting into action?*

an adult Christian will not be relevant to the situations in which the children find themselves.

I became acutely aware of this some years ago when a friend of mine, eleven years old at the time, telephoned me. He had recently started at a secondary school and, being a Christian of such devotion that it puts me to shame, determined that he would witness there to his faith in God. His reason for phoning was that he had been thrown down a flight of fourteen concrete stairs. I know there were fourteen because he was in such distress that I decided to go to see him straightaway, even though it was a distance of a hundred miles or so. I counted them — fourteen, bottom to top.

At his church they had taught him, quite rightly, that it is the Christian's duty to tell others about Christ. What they had omitted to do was discuss with him how he might go about it when he was the only Christian in a school of more than a thousand. I can see what went on in his head! He thought, 'Who in this school needs most to be converted to following Jesus? Of course — the school bully!' So he had gone up to him, given him a tract and told him to pray. It was inevitable that he would be thrown down the stairs, wasn't it?

I spent a considerable amount of time with him talking about what he could actually achieve for Jesus, given those circumstances. I listened as he described the school, shared my own experience, but made sure that it was he who decided what was possible and what was too risky. In fact he decided that he would not tell anyone that he was a Christian for two terms. He would use the time to build up real friendships, and only then would he look for opportunities to show those who had come to like and trust him that he had a faith in God. I don't know whether his decision was right or wrong. My task was not to speculate on that, but to help him see the implications of the course he chose, pray about it with him, and then to prompt him to stick to it. This was a lot more difficult than just telling him what to do, with the bluntness of a Christmas cracker motto — but it was time that I have never regretted spending.

It is clear that what God expects of his followers differs according to their ages. For example, while Paul's advice, 'Open your homes to strangers' (Romans 12:13) is a good exhortation to give to young adults, it would be totally irresponsible to suggest it to children. Equally it is obvious that the activities with which you help children to work out the implications of what they have learnt will vary from age to age. It is the leader's task to gauge what is right and adapt activities to fit.

## Holding a discussion

Almost all children are used to taking part in discussions at school. As part of learning to communicate, they are encouraged from a very early age to express their own opinions. Many schoolteachers are skilled at leading discussions in a way which does not allow talkative children to dominate, and it is good to emulate them. Start when children are as young as possible by asking questions which make them think for themselves. It is of little value to ask questions to which the answers are always, 'Yes', 'No', or 'Jesus'! Instead, ask questions about feelings and decisions. For example, rather than asking, 'Who let Jesus down by pretending that he did not even know him?' you could ask, 'How do you think Peter felt after he had lied about knowing Jesus?' Here is the conversation that might follow:

'What words would you use to describe the feelings Peter had?'

Several hands go up and David bellows out an answer. 'There's no need to shout out David. I'll get round to you in a moment, because I've got loads of time and I can listen to everybody. Sally, what do you think?'

'Ashamed of himself,' suggests Sally.

'Yes, I think he probably was. Well done! David, what did you want to say?'

'Pleased to get out of danger.'

'I should think there was an element of that too. Thank you for suggesting it.' You notice Scott, who would never push himself forward. 'What do you think, Scott?'

Scott whispers, 'Bad.'

'Bad!' You repeat it to make sure that the others heard. 'I'm sure he did. Good answer! Anyone else?' Winston puts up his hand.

'Serve him right.'

'That's an interesting answer.' You're not quite sure what he means. You don't want to discourage him by making him feel stupid, but you don't want to agree with anything that might be contrary to what we know about the Bible. 'What do the others think about that?'

'Well he didn't want to get into trouble,' suggests David, 'but he probably felt worse than if he had told the truth.'

'That's certainly true. Is that more or less what you meant, Winston?'

'Yes.'

Phew! Laura hasn't spoken yet. 'Have you got any ideas Laura?' There is a silence. Laura is obviously very embarrassed, so you need to help out. 'Do you think he felt miserable or OK?'

'Miserable!'

'Yes, I'll bet he did. Thanks, Laura.' And so it goes on.

As the children grow older, it is possible to have discussions which are more wide-ranging. Suppose that, with nine year olds, you have been looking at Jesus' teaching that his followers should 'turn the other cheek' (Matthew 5:39). If you tell children that this means they should never fight in the playground, you must be aware that you are commanding something very, very hard for some children. In certain areas, fighting is deeply ingrained in the culture and children may be taught at home that it is morally wrong to walk away from an attack.

It would be more valuable to start a discussion by asking, 'Is it ever right to fight in the playground?' If a child says something which you feel to be wrong, to tell him so bluntly is unfair because your greater intellect and ability with words will always ensure that you 'win'. Instead, ask whether any others in the group have a different opinion. If all the group share one opinion, whether or not you think it is a good opinion, that is a good time to challenge them by referring to passages in the Bible and asking whether they consider these have any part to play in the decision, and why. You could follow up the discussion by making a list of all the possible alternatives, including fighting, which present themselves in that situation. Think briefly about the strengths and weaknesses of each, then have a short silence during which children can consider whether God is telling them how they might behave in the future. Then it is up to you to go home and pray that the Holy Spirit will lead the children — and their parents — into the truth.

Sometimes it is a big help to start a discussion with some decision-making that everyone can be involved in. For instance, you might want to discuss how Christians should behave towards those of other faiths. You could split the group into pairs and give each pair a set of cards to sort into two piles — good reactions and bad reactions. The cards might bear the words, 'befriend them, tell them to go to another country, stick up for them, find out about their customs, pray for them, insult them, join in with their worship, keep a distance so there is no trouble . . .' and so on. After leaving children to work by themselves for a few minutes, begin the discussion by comparing the way the pairs have arranged their cards. 'Tom and Jay, you thought it was good to find out about the customs of people you know from other faiths, but Jacquie and Liz, you thought that was bad for Christians to do. Why's that?'

One warning — while it is extremely good training in a democracy to take a vote after a discussion on 'Where should we go for our annual outing?', it is never a good idea after discussions on matters of doctrine. Votes suggest that one side or other have 'won'. That is not what you are seeking at all. Instead you are hoping that each child will decide before God what is right and what is wrong — and choose of his own free will what he will do in response.

## Craft work

There is a temptation to think of craft work as a time filler or a way of keeping children happy. It is more than that — it is a tool that can be used to help children relate Christianity to their own lives.

### Drawing and colouring

At the younger end of children's work, these will probably be the most frequent creative activities. They are easy to organize, so do not despise them, but don't overdo them either. To ask children to draw a Bible story is an obvious use of craft work — it is fun to draw Mary pouring perfume over Jesus' feet. A more imaginative use of drawing would be to say, 'Mary gave Jesus the perfume simply to make him happy. Draw yourself doing something that you could do tomorrow to make Jesus really happy.'

On the whole, drawing has more educational value than colouring (although colouring is useful for increasing children's hand-eye coordination and attention to detail, the value of which need not be ignored just because you run a Sunday School, not a day school). If you are giving children pictures of Bible stories to colour, make sure that they are accurate to the text so that children do not reinforce wrong ideas about the Bible. You should, for example, think twice about giving children pictures to colour which show Bible characters with European features, rather than Middle Eastern ones.

When selecting equipment, there is a choice to be made. Children prefer the bright colours of felt-tipped pens, but coloured pencils last many times longer. If you choose the former, discipline the group into putting the lids on the pens to stop them drying out (simply don't let them start the next activity or go home until they have done so). If you choose the latter, discipline them into sharpening the crayons over the waste paper basket, not the floor!

Show that you value what they create by displaying it on the wall in a neat, symmetrical arrangement with a caption. Display all their efforts, not just the best. In this way, you show them that God values the creative things they do in response to him, and has no favourites. Arrange the display on or below the children's eye level (not your own). Change it every few weeks and draw attention to it regularly. Do I need to say, 'Never give a child a torn piece of paper to draw on'? Well, I've said it anyway!

## Pictures and friezes
You need not be restricted to felt-tipped pens. Children can create pictures from pieces of material, different sorts of coloured and textured paper, mosaic squares cut from magazines — these are all known as collage. A similar technique called montage involves cutting out photographs, children's drawings or headlines from newspapers and arranging them in a pattern which illustrates a particular theme with words and pictures. Older children could use this technique to say what they feel about the beauty of creation, violence, purposelessness, love and so on.

For both techniques you need a large sheet of paper as a background — the end of a roll of plain wallpaper is suitable, anything from a craft shop is expensive. Choose scissors carefully. Round-ended scissors are best for young children, but are frustrating for cutting anything heavier than paper. More accidents are caused with blunt scissors than sharp ones, so be warned. And how about keeping a pair of left-handed scissors to show a child who usually struggles that you (and God) care enough to bother! Buy paste ready-mixed in small containers (a huge pot may be better value, but it's hopeless when ten children need it at once) or, better still, as a stick. Don't expect miracles from lightweight paste — it will not stick fabrics satisfactorily. For those you will need to use rubber solution glue and, since that can be abused like any other solvent, you should do so with care.

If you don't have tables to use for this, buy some pieces of hardboard for children to rest on their knees. If you cannot afford hardboard, use flattened grocery boxes. If that is inconvenient, ask the children to kneel on the floor and work on the seats of their chairs. If you haven't got chairs, get some!

## Modelling

Making models appeals to a lot of children who recognize that it requires less precise artistic talent than drawing. *Plasticine* is a good material since it can be reused if it is stored in an airtight container. Dough made from 3kg flour, 1kg salt and a little water is a cheap alternative. Pipe cleaner figures are endlessly adaptable and can be made to stand up if they are pushed into polystyrene tiles. Puppets are fun and can be used to retell the Bible story, or improvise a modern-day drama. The easiest puppets are made from a wooden spoon with a face drawn on the bowl and a piece of material tied around the neck. Every variation on this, using cardboard tubes, paper bags or even dressing up your own fingers, is possible. The experienced Sunday School leader treasures other peoples' rubbish! Never let a friend throw away a shoebox if you think the children can make it into a synagogue!

I have often used paint in a Sunday School and never once done so without regretting it half an hour after the children have gone, when I am still trying to scrape it out of the carpet. You have to weigh the joy of the children against the hassle factor! Now go and prove me wrong!

*Think big?*

## Drama and case studies

Many people are put off drama by their memories of cute children in dressing gowns reciting from scripts to adoring parents. Forget it! That's not drama — it's putting on a show, which is equally valuable in its own way, but not part of a Sunday School's life.

To get best value out of drama, think small, and abandon the idea that it has to be shown to anyone. Start while the children are still young by getting them to think themselves into a Bible story. You might get them to stomp across the room as Goliath — all of them, so that no one has to settle for a small part and watch the 'star'. Then ask them all to be David, moving around the room, imagining that the huge man is only yards from them. How do they feel? Can they put it into words? Then tell the whole story, with all the children expressing emotions and actions after each sentence.

As children grow older, the use to which drama can be put becomes more significant. It is possible for children to improvise little scenes for themselves which allow them to discover what it feels like to put a Christian principle into

101

practice. For example, suppose you were considering the story of Joseph and Potiphar's wife (Genesis 39) in order to find out how God wants Christians to react when they are unjustly accused. After telling the story and drawing some conclusions from it, you could use drama to give children a chance to experiment with Christian responses. Put the children into pairs and ask one of them to play the part of a school teacher and one to play a child. They are to improvize a scene in which the teacher reprimands the child for doing something of which the child is innocent (not a rare occurrence!). All the pairs do this at once, since they are not performing for anyone else (although the leaders could move from pair to pair, watching, encouraging and making suggestions). After that, tell them to swop roles and act the scene again, trying to bring it to a different, even more satisfactory, conclusion. This will allow them to experiment with what it feels like to act in a godly way, but with the assurance that they are in a completely safe setting. A 'dry run' will leave them better prepared for next time it happens in real life.

It is important not to give up after the first try, which is almost certain to be shaky, since children take time to learn how to do this.

Another way to explore the same ground with children is to show them realistic 'case studies' and ask them how they would react. For example, after studying Daniel, you might be discussing how to stand up for what is right. You could ask several different groups each to choose at random a sealed envelope containing a problem. They are to talk about it together, before reporting back to the rest. (The envelopes aren't obligatory — they just add to the excitement and prove that you were not getting at any child in particular.) One of them might contain this case study. 'Your class has been left unsupervised in the classroom while the teacher has gone to answer an urgent phone call. One of the class has started to read out rude bits from a tabloid newspaper. Everyone is listening and laughing, but a couple of your friends are looking at you to see how you react. What would you do?'

Again, this is not an uncommon situation for children in the final years of primary school. The feature which makes it a good case study is that there is no cut-and-dried correct answer. There are many possible responses, some of which children could do easily and some of which would take outstanding courage. The leader should not tell the children the right thing to do (which might lead to great stress), but could gently challenge the agreed solution. If the group gives a trite, virtuous answer, you could go on to ask how they would cope with the derision that would certainly come from the rest of the class. If the suggested solution is not to take any action at all, ask what difference it makes that the children are representing Christ in that classroom.

This technique could be combined with discussion or with drama. Like both of those, it relies on the leader leaving children free to decide, on the basis of all the evidence, what is practical for them to do in response to their desire to please God — neither prompted by guilt to make big resolutions that will end in failure, nor lulled into inaction by the inability to see any connection between the Bible and their own lives!

## Testimonies

There is a great range of Christian experience in your own congregation from which the children can benefit. It is good for children to see that the Christian life works in practice for all sorts of adults and teenagers, not just for their familiar Sunday School leaders. It is especially important for boys to meet Christian men who are proud of their faith (unless there is a miraculous change over the next few months in the ratio of male to female leaders in children's groups). If they do not, there is a danger that they will grow up believing that Christianity is for women and children. All Christian children need to see Christian adults of whom they can think, 'I wouldn't mind being like that!'

Choose carefully those whom you invite to talk about their lives as Christians. It is vital to discuss before the event what the person will say, so that you can be sure it is appropriate to the age and understanding of the children you know. You will probably decide that an interview is preferable to a monologue. It means that you can control the length and, to some extent, the content. It helps to keep the testimony light-hearted, but make sure that the serious points do not go for nothing. It also helps enormously if the person to whom the children are introduced has got a certain amount of street-cred!

## Learning parts of the Bible

This has been much-maligned recently, but I would be sorry to see it go altogether. It has been valuable for me, and I can't be the only one! Quite a lot of bits and pieces of the Bible have stuck in my mind over the years and I can't remember which I learned deliberately. However, one verse that I know I made a point of learning has come back to me again and again at crisis points — 'I acted differently because I honoured God' (Nehemiah 5:15). Last month that verse was solely responsible for stopping me leaving a car park without putting my money in the honesty-box, although unfortunately it did not stop the rather rude word that flashed through my brain when I reversed into it, trying to get close enough to avoid getting out of the car.

Select the verse you ask the children to learn with some care — it must be one that really will be useful to them in ten, twenty, fifty years. Some sentences in the Bible were originally designed to be committed to memory. For example, God commanded the people of Israel to memorize these words, 'I created you to be my servant and I will never forget you. . . . Come back to me; I am the one who saves you' (Isaiah 44:21–22). 2500 years later there are still no words that we could better ask adults and children alike to pack into the corners of their memories against the day when they need to be reminded that they are precious to God. Perhaps verses like that should head the list.

Here is some quick fire advice! Make sure that the leaders learn the verse alongside the children. Explain what the reference of a verse is and how to use it to find the words in a Bible (I call it 'the address' instead of the reference). Be consistent in the way you state the chapter and verse. Revise a verse regularly for a month and occasionally over the rest of a year, or it will soon be forgotten. Above all, make it fun by presenting it with codes, puzzles, jigsaws, anagrams, and games — it all helps!

## Work sheets

Whoops! I've used a schoolroom word! It's better to call them fun sheets or quiz sheets. If they seem like work to the children, they may have lost their value.

Sheets like these can be used in many ways. They can be used to revise a Bible story in an entertaining way, with puzzles and quizzes. This is particularly valuable if it makes the children want to look at a Bible to solve a particular clue. It allows them to realize that the story comes from Scripture and is not just invented. This is good training for them, since we hope that one day they will take their practical and spiritual problems to the Bible to look for guidance or solutions.

If you are devising your own fun sheets, look at a children's puzzle magazine in a newsagent before you start, and find out what kinds of puzzle boys and girls attempt for their own amusement. You will notice that there is a strong visual

105

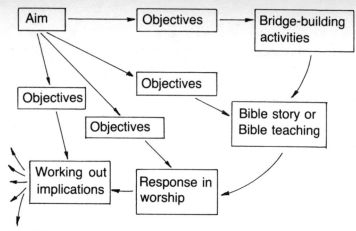

*The aim, objectives and programme now look like this.*

appeal to the puzzles — either pictures or a good deal of design. Try to emulate this, and certainly look for it if you are choosing one of the many Sunday School schemes that are on the market.

Fun sheets, though, can also provide a direct link between the content of the Bible and its implications for day to day life. Children can be asked to complete pictures to show what they would do in certain situations, or to finish a prayer which makes the teaching personal. They can write captions to cartoons with subtle meanings, or put expressions on faces to show how they would feel about doing certain things.

It is crucial, though, to get the level of interest correct for the age-group at which you are aiming the material. Seeing a work sheet brings out all my sympathy for children who find them tough at school. It must feel dreadful to come to church and find more of the same sense of failure. My tendency is to err on the side of the non-reader, rather than the know-it-all. Whenever it is possible for the children to draw a response, rather than write it, specify that they have a choice. Favour mazes and join-the-dot puzzles over anagrams and elaborate codes.

Think big, think visual, think fun! Just think!

# Things to do

**1** Think of one of the children in your group with all of his or her family. Read Ephesians 6:1–4. In your mind, picture the family doing things which show the verses you have just read being put into practice.

**2** Now imagine that you are leading a Sunday School session which has involved learning from those verses. After the main teaching, you intend to ask children to take part in an artistic acitivity and produce something which shows them putting what they have learnt into action. There are many ways of approaching it — drawing, colouring, modelling, collage, and so on. Knowing your own group and the facilities available to you, what materials would you provide in this case?

**3** Think of a situation that your chosen family might get into which could either end in anger and distress, or in reconciliation and peace. Write it out, as though you were going to give it to little groups of children as a case study to work out satisfactorily or a drama to improvise and bring to a godly conclusion.

**4** Choose the five or six most important words in the passage. Arrange them so that they interlink like a crossword. Think of some simple clues which would give these words as answers. The clues should refer to the verses the children have read.

**5** Draw a picture of the family you chose having a row. Put a piece of greaseproof paper over the top of it. Trace the picture, but make nine or ten changes so that the copy shows the family at peace, having sorted out the argument. Make some of the alterations obvious and some really detailed. If your drawing is awful, hide it somewhere and have another practice. If it is reasonable, give it to a child and ask him or her to spot the differences.

# 9
# Making friends with children

I've just been trying to remember what the Sunday School I grew up in was like. I'm quite shocked by how little I can remember — a few vague recollections of a prefabricated hall and the noise when it rained. I certainly cannot remember any Bible story I learnt there for the first time, although I am sure I heard many. I have only two distinct memories. The first one is of the wooden chairs we sat on. It was before the days of little furniture for little people, and my legs would dangle in mid-air until they went to sleep, week after week.

The second memory is of my Sunday School leader. Her name was Naomi and I used to think she was wonderful. But in my mind I don't connect her with the church hall — I remember her so well because she took me ten pin bowling! I used to think this was the best fun in the whole of creation. And that's where I learnt my Christianity — there among the pin-ball machines and juke boxes! It never bothered me that I couldn't see Jesus in person — I could see Naomi, and if she said that God was watching the evening I bowled my first strike, there was no reason to disagree!

It is both an encouragement and a daunting prospect for

leaders like us that, no matter how often we talk about Joshua, Jacob or Jesus, it is the relationship we have with those who are listening that tells the children most about Christianity. Just think what children learn about God if the person who represents him to them is caring, fair, welcoming and anxious for their well-being. On the other hand, be warned of what the children learn about God if the adults who talk about him shout at them, show no interest in their lives, or disappear for weeks on end because they take the Sunday School on a rota!

Children in churches need leaders, but more than that they need friends. That applies to the disgruntled teenager as much as to the vulnerable toddler. Don't get me wrong — they don't need adults who pretend to be chummy, they need friends! The value of grown-up friends is that they can be role models, counsellors and advisers — but the greatest value of grown-up friends is that they can be friends!

It has always puzzled me that some adults have difficulty in making genuine friendships with children. It is not so very different from forming friendships with adults — perhaps the difficulty is that we expect it to be different. We get so used to telling children important things that we forget to listen to what they are saying to us. If only we could learn to listen to children! God might have such thrilling things to say through them. Just imagine if the Jewish teachers in the Temple had been so determined to explain their religion to the twelve-year-old Jesus that they had not taken time to listen. They would have missed the chance to converse with God himself. Fortunately for them, they had the sensitivity to listen to what Jesus was saying, and not surprisingly 'all who heard him were amazed at his intelligent answers' (Luke 2:47). Of course, we will never have the young Jesus playing beside us on a volleyball court, nor even contributing to a discussion group, but don't forget that he said, 'Whoever welcomes in my name one of these children, welcomes me' (Mark 9:37).

# Seven things that children see right through

Everyone's experience of befriending children is different. I can only offer some of the things I have learnt from the past. Here are a few of the mistakes I have made — and don't want to make again!

## Using a strange tone of voice

There is no special children's voice, despite anything you might hear from children's entertainers or on the television. Performers want specific reactions from children — admiration, excitement or something similar. Their objectives are nothing to do with long-term friendship, and there is no need for them to listen to children, merely to impress them. There is nothing wrong with that, but children recognize it for what it is. The voice to which children respond with trust, confidence and affection is the one you use with the greengrocer and your neighbour.

## Making every question a Bible question

If all you ever talk about with children is related to the Bible, or designed to lead up to direct evangelism, what will they make of you? They will probably draw the conclusion that you are only interested in their soul, not the whole of them — although they wouldn't use those particular words to describe the problem. At worst it can lead to children switching off to everything you have to say — at a dubious best it leads to children giving you the answers you want to hear, just to please you.

One of my colleagues tells a story about a Sunday School she visited where a leader was talking with a group of five-year-old children about the wonder of God's creation. 'Now, who can tell me what I am thinking of?' she asked. 'It's grey, it's furry, it's got a long fluffy tail and it eats nuts.'

Several hands went up and she chose a little boy to answer. 'Well,' he said hesitantly, 'I know the answer *must* be Jesus, but it sounds to me awfully like a squirrel.'

Anyone can produce children who use the right religious words, but to form a friendship which leads to honesty, children need to know that they have the freedom to talk about anything at all.

## Lack of interest in children's replies

Children need to know that their opinion matters. They need to see you think about what they say and react to it. That may involve asking questions and, when the children have answered, asking others which show interest and uncover more detail or more feelings. It may even involve changing your plans if the children's answers show that what you had in mind is not appropriate.

I once watched an elderly Sunday School leader ask her young group to choose the hymn they would like to sing next.

'Praise him, praise him,' said a girl, grinning with satisfaction that she had been chosen.

'No, it's not that one,' said the leader. The girl sank back in her chair, confused.

'Jesus' love is very wonderful,' requested a boy.

'No, it's not that one either,' replied the lady, provoking more disappointment.

This was repeated four or five times until a child chose 'All things bright and beautiful'.

'Yes that's the one,' said the leader, turning to me contentedly. 'They always choose the right one sooner or later.'

I bit my lip!

## Towering above children

When I was young I had an Uncle Leslie who was mayor of some obscure town in the West Country. For all I know he may still be alive, in which case I apologize for telling a story at his expense. He must have been over one metre ninety tall, but from my eye-level, round about his thigh, he might as well have stretched up for kilometres. He wore his chain of office almost continually, and when he spoke to me, he clasped his hands behind his back and bent at the waist until he reached a perfect right angle. That still left his face some distance above mine, and his gold chain used to dangle right in front of my nose. It's quite possible that he was the nicest man in the whole of Devon! I shall never know, because I can't picture his face or remember anything he said — all I can recall is that chain swaying threateningly backwards and forwards, reducing me to a shy silence.

The way to make children comfortable in conversation is to place yourself on or below their eye-level. It means that you are not imposing your opinions and subjects for conversation on to them because of your superior height. Personally, I recommend slouching, but before physiotherapists rise up against me in their thousands, I ought to add that there are other ways!

As children grow through their teens, the problem lessens. The difficulty is with younger children. It presents itself particularly when they are sitting at low tables drawing or writing. If, when you approach to encourage them, you stand or bend over beside them, you make it physically difficult for them to address you. If you sit or crouch beside them so that your eyes are below theirs, you find yourself drawn into *their* conversation, without any effort.

## Getting the level of sophistication wrong

Have a guess at which UK television show is watched by the largest number of children in the seven to eleven age range. Before you let your thoughts range over the excellent programmes made specifically for children, let me cut short your speculation. It is *Neighbours*, the adult soap opera. If you have watched it, you will be aware of the range of adult problems and experiences which it opens up to children at a young age. Even those who never watch it almost certainly talk about it in the playground. One of my school children, ten years old, once asked me what it means to be 'on the game'. 'Good grief!' I replied, taken off-guard. 'Wherever did you hear that expression?' It turned out to be on one of the early evening soap operas. Of course, I answered his question in a low-key way — I couldn't damage our relationship by making it seem as though I knew 'secret, wicked things' which I needed to hide from him. But I was sad to do so, very sad, because it meant that there was one tiny bit of innocence less in the life of a smashing kid.

If you make the assumption that a thirteen-year-old girl is

interested in dolls, when in fact she has a boyfriend, there is a risk that she will not talk to you about either. If she does have a boyfriend, she will almost certainly need advice or a pattern to follow — and if she doesn't get that from an older Christian friend, there are plenty of less helpful models in the world for her to copy.

## Talking to the parent over the head of the child

We've all done it! 'Would he like a *Coke*?' you ask the parent, while the child is standing right beside you, perfectly capable of making his own decision.

It might be worth considering to whom you send letters when occasion demands that a note is sent from the Sunday School to the home. Do you, for example, send an invitation to a Christmas party to the child whom you hope will come, or to her parents? Knowing how much children love receiving letters, my guess is that you should send it to the child. Of course, you risk the possibility that the news will never reach the parent, but you can always find a way around that with personal contact or an acceptance slip to be returned.

## Pretending you're a big kid really!

This is the lesson I learnt hardest and least willingly. There is a very seductive possibility, particularly with young teenagers, of pretending that you can roll back the years and be just like them. It took me a long time to realize that you can wear the clothes, you can speak the language, you can play the games, but a fourteen year old recognizes an adult in disguise within ten seconds.

The fault is lack of confidence! If you assume that a child can only make friends with someone who is a pseudo-child, you are missing the point! Children want friendship, and for that genuine article they are prepared to accept all kinds of differences and age gaps. A far better route than forcing your way into a child's world is to offer him or her a place in your world. That way you can achieve real friendship, not just become 'a good laugh'. Joining in a bundle on the carpet is a short-term giggle, but asking a child to come with you to the warehouse and help you choose a new carpet for your sitting room builds a long-term trust. Having a water fight

113

on the grass shows a child that you can still have fun after all these years, but asking a child to help you mow the lawn shows him that you need him as well as appreciate him. The difference becomes obvious three or four years on!

## Seven things that children respond to well

I have found that these actions help to build long-term relationships with children.

### Sharing your feelings with children
If you want children to confide in you, then you must confide in them. Children do not intuitively discover how to get the most out of friendship — they learn by copying. Obviously, you must match what you confide in children to what their emotional development can cope with — there is no point in asking for their sympathy in an area which they are too young to understand.

All Sunday School leaders know that they should pray for their children, but for some reason, far fewer ask children to pray for them. As years go on, it is possible to reveal much more to children about what makes you happy or sad or fearful. It will not help them in the slightest to grow up thinking that Christian adults are invulnerable. If they do, the rude awakening they get may make them ask negative questions about God.

### Demonstrating trust
It is not only valuable, but a Christian principle, that we should build up each others' self esteem. For children, one of the ways in which this happens is for them to show they are capable of fulfilling trust that has been placed in them. It is good to take every opportunity to let children do difficult things unaided in order to help you — although once again, you will need to take great care that you are not stretching them beyond their capability at a particular age, or placing temptations in their way which are unfairly strong.

The sort of help I have in mind is, instead of asking 'Would you like a drink?' requesting, 'Could you go and make me a coffee?' At a younger age, you could ask a girl to

114

operate the cassette recorder when you are listening to a Christian song. At an older age, you could ask a boy to count up and bag the money given in the collection. All of these involve taking a risk — that is the whole point of the exercise! You risk the cassette being dropped or the money being stolen, but you potentially gain the respect and increased maturity of the child. The skill is to know where to draw the line.

Some time ago when I went on holiday, I gave one of my school children a key to my flat and asked him to let himself in and water my plants. I went away with only moderate expectations. I need not have worried! Those plants didn't know what had hit them — they got better treatment that week than the orchids at Kew. When I got back the flat had been dusted and vacuumed throughout. I never bothered to ask for the key back!

## Spending 'quality time' with children

'Quality time' is time when listening and talking to children is the main point of the exercise, not the by-product when you are busy doing something else. I know a church where all the men took all the boys fishing on a lazy spring afternoon. I've no idea whether they caught anything — I only know that the boys still talk about it eighteen months later. I don't think they were intent on being sexist — they were just deliberately working on what they identified to be the relationship in their families most likely to be squeezed during their busy lives.

My hunch is that there is little to be gained in the long-term from giving children expensive treats. Anyone can spend money on children! But it takes someone special to set aside time for them in a loving way.

## Being up to date with children's interests

Let's face it, you are asking children to share your interest in Christianity — the least you can do is to reciprocate. One of the differences between your interest and the children's is that Christianity changes slowly and God never — children's interests change month by month. To flick through children's magazines when you are in the newsagent buying a paper

115

will reveal a lot in a few minutes. Watching some children's television occasionally will help, and you ought to know the names of the local sports teams, toys that are being advertised widely, and rock groups that are in vogue. It doesn't matter if you do not know much detail about them — that, after all, gives you something to find out from children in conversation.

## Remembering and developing

If you are able to recall from one conversation to another what you have discovered about children, it shows them that what they have said is important to you. It is difficult for them to be confident that you are listening if you ask them what school they go to every time you chat. Ask them about events that they are looking forward to, or dreading, then find out at a later date what happened and how they felt about it all.

## Finding ways of telling children that you like them

This may be the hardest of all the things I have suggested. It ought not to be, but I understand why it is.

Children need to know that they are special, especially in their mid-teens, when to imagine yourself disliked or ignored is not uncommon. Curiously it is teenagers, who most need to hear that they are liked, who are least likely to accept the compliment. Very often, to declare the complete opposite, 'I really hate your guts!' with a broad grin is more likely to get the message home. In other cases, where to say, 'You're a good friend! Thanks!' is inappropriate, you will need to show it by putting yourself out on a child's behalf and hoping that the reasons for doing so sink in.

In this, and all the other points, it is worth remembering that as well as children who are instantly likeable you are always bound to know children who are not. It is good to be sure that you have not just conveniently left out of your thinking children who don't fit the ideal mould.

## Helping out in conversation

Conversation is a skill which children need to learn just as painstakingly as learning to tie shoelaces or drop a backhand lob on to the base line. Rather than leaving them to struggle as they try to talk to you, it is possible to help them out.

You can make conversation easier for children by asking them open-ended questions. Closed questions are those to which there is only one set of answers, and they usually end a conversation. For example:

'Do you like your school?'

'Yes.'

End!

Open-ended questions are those which present almost limitless possibilities for an answer, and they enlarge a conversation. For instance:

'What are your favourite things about school?'

To that question, there may well be half a dozen answers, each of which can open out into a chat about the way children feel about their lives.

At a meal-time, instead of asking an eight-year-old, 'Do you like it?' you could ask, 'If you could choose your best meal, what would you have?' The first question closes the conversation. The second throws open endless possibilities and also helps you to listen to the answer, not just wait for the response you expect.


## Finally, a warning

I am sorry to have to give this warning, but our society is changing and to leave it unsaid would be unwise.

Children need to know that they are safe with adults. Parents need to know that their sons and daughters are safe too. There is a great deal of damage done to children by adults, both intentionally and unintentionally. Even in churches it is vital to err on the side of caution for their safety. It would deprive the church of one of the great positive values of Christianity if adults were never able to touch children, but it must not be misinterpreted. The wisest approach is to enjoy hugging and holding and scrapping with children right out in the open where everyone is watching happily and no one can misunderstand what is going on. It is when adults

117

insist these things must be secret that children become concerned, sometimes with good reason.

It is also important that parents are kept completely informed about the relationships other adults are forming with their children. In nearly every case, the loving concern of a Sunday School leader will be welcomed, and it is usually a matter of joy to tell parents what is going on in their children's lives — provided you can do so without betraying particular confidences which children have placed in you.

How sad to have to finish the chapter with a warning like this! But the world can be a cruel place for children — that is part of the nature of mankind and Jesus had to come to earth to deal with it. Not to mention it would be to forget the very reason that adults and children alike need to turn to God for forgiveness.

## Things to do

**1** List all the children in your group in a column on the left hand side of a sheet, and draw vertical lines to create five other columns.

**2** Next to each name, write down a particular interest that the child has about which you could talk to him or her at any time.

**3** In the next column, write down how long ago you had a conversation with that child more substantial than, 'Hallo, have you had a good week?' or an instruction to do with the Sunday School programme.

**4** Fourthly, write a way in which you could make that particular boy or girl feel special, valued or trusted in the next few weeks.

**5** Next, put a tick if the child knows roughly as much about you as you know about him or her. Put a cross against any to whom you are a virtual stranger.

**6** Finally, in the right hand column, put a tick if the child is one whom you particularly like. Examine whether it is true that, while you have developed a good relationship with those children you like, your answers have revealed that your relationship with the others could be better.

**7** Your answers will almost certainly have brought to light things which you need to thank God for and others that you ought to pray about. Plan how you will pray individually for every child on your list in the coming week.

# 10
# The girl who feared a heart transplant

'I've asked Jesus into my heart,' said Cassie, who was ten years old.

She knew how to pick her moments! I was underneath a washing-up machine trying to work out why it was smearing the custard round the dishes, not removing it. There were fifty boys and girls staying in a boarding school near Bristol on a children's Christian holiday. 'That's terrific,' I said. 'I think you have made the best decision you will ever make.'

'Oh not just now,' she said, 'years ago!'

I found the switch and injected soap into the machine.

'Peter,' hesitated Cassie, 'you know the heart transplants at Papworth Hospital?'

'Yes,' I replied, because the newspapers were full of them at that time.

'If ever I have a heart transplant, will I need to invite Jesus into my new heart too?'

It took me a long time to realize what a sensible question she was asking — it was the best way she had of understanding the information she had been given. It was the adults who had spoken to her over the years about the Christian faith who should have known better.

## Can a child be a Christian?

The difficulty that children have in understanding religious language has led some people to suggest that children cannot be Christians in the full sense of the word. I think they are wrong, but their opinions are valuable because they make us think hard. In this, as in every other matter of doctrine, the first place to look for help is in the life of Christ.

Those who see Christianity as a uniquely adult faith often forget that God chose to allow Jesus to grow from a baby to a child to a man in a family. He need not have! Jesus could have appeared as a grown man at his baptism or in the wilderness — but speculation is idle, because he didn't. He was once a boy!

And he was a complete, real boy, as well as being totally God. There is never a suggestion that Jesus was less than fully God when he was a child. It was not a period when he was on probation for becoming divine. Paul tells us that 'the full content of divine nature lives in Christ, in his humanity' (Colossians 2:9). It is quite true, but it must not lead us to be superstitious about the nature of Jesus' childhood. It is tempting to think that he had the body of a three-year-old, but the mind of a perfect adult. Not so! At the age of five he was making the kind of relationships that other five-year-olds in Judaea were making — but he was making them perfectly. At the age of eight he had the relationship with God the Father that was appropriate for a perfect eight-year-old to have. It was absolutely unique, but it was not the same as a perfect adult relationship with God — it couldn't be, he was still a boy! This is what it means when people talk about 'incarnation'.

What God wants for a child is that he or she should be as much like the child Jesus at the same age as it is possible for a sinful human to be. It is what we should want too. If you believe that Jesus was fully human, you have to believe that a child can fully be accepted in the Kingdom of God.

# An example, for what it's worth!

It is time to give you a few paragraphs from my biography. It is the incomparable privilege of my life that I have never known a day in it when I have not been aware of God's love for me and my love for him. I was baptized and taken to church practically from birth by faithful parents. At the age of eight I remember being taken to Billy Graham's mission in London and saying, 'You know, I'm a friend of Jesus too,' much to the evident thrill of those around me. At eleven I went to the Christian Union at secondary school and heard the story of the lost son, which suddenly I understood and responded to as never before. At twenty I began to lead the youth club in my church and through working alongside and observing my friend Chris realized that I was going to have to take following Christ a whole lot more seriously if I was going to be any use to him at all. Then, in October of 1987, I was licensed as a lay reader in the Anglican church, and committed myself to serving God with a depth that I wouldn't have thought was possible ten years ago.

So which one of those was my conversion? None of them ... well, all of them ... I don't know! I can't tell, because each one means as much to me as the rest — and I have a feeling that God has not finished with me yet!

In contrast, friends of mine have come to a faith in God after years of complete ignorance of or apathy towards him. Many of them found no encouragement at all from their families, but can put a specific date on the occasion when God confirmed that he had accepted them into his kingdom as Christians. For some this happened as a child, for some as an adult. The experience seems to have been equally valid for both. In nearly all these cases (and certainly in all those who entrusted themselves to Christ as a child) another adult was involved, either explaining the faith or living a life of such worth that they were prompted to find the cause. They speak of it in many different ways — 'being born again', 'giving my life to Christ', 'entering the kingdom of God'. Of course, all their descriptions are metaphors, but from the way they talk you know that the experience was not metaphorical — it was real! To use Peter's straight-talking explanation, 'at one time they were not God's people, but now they are his people' (1 Peter 2:10).

## Are 'conversion' metaphors helpful?

Yes and no! They didn't help Cassie, whose story opened the chapter, because she took them literally — but even that did not stop God being gracious. The fact is that it is impossible to talk about God without using metaphors — he is so great that literal language breaks down. The best we can do is to choose the metaphor carefully, be consistent in the way we use it, and talk practically about what commitment means to the way we live our lives.

For young children, 'belonging to God' is a helpful way to describe being a Christian. After all, they have toys and pets which belong to them, so they understand the concept. It also has the virtue of stressing that grace is a matter of what God has done for us, not what we do for God. Within that, it is possible to talk about 'loving and obeying Jesus' or 'being a friend of Jesus' as a description of our responsibilities.

As a teenager I was helping at a holiday club when a five-year-old boy asked me, 'Are you Jesus?' Years later I still regret that the question took me by surprise and I did not have a proper answer ready. Nowadays I make sure that children discover some facts about the historical Jesus as a first priority, so I don't suppose the question will ever arise again — but I can't help hoping that the boy found someone else who could sort out his confusion for him.

It is unwise to talk to young children about the part the cross played in making them acceptable to God. They simply cannot take in what atonement means until they are more mature. Of course, it is right to tell them that Jesus died and rose again (never separating the two), but to ask them to comprehend the language of sacrifice or the language of victory would be damaging. It is enough to tell the boys and girls of this age, 'You can say sorry to Jesus.' After all, if they belong to Christ, he died for them, redeemed them and rose to inaugurate their new, forgiven life *whether they understand it or not.*

The older children get, the more it is possible to explain what God has done for them in Christ, and the response he asks of them. However, you need to remember that children do not think in abstract ways until they are fourteen or more. Ideas like 'sin' and 'justice' need to be spelled out with examples. If you are building on a background of Bible teaching and application, then there is less risk of confusing children.

In these circumstances you need to question and talk personally with a child, fully discussing what it is going to mean in practical terms to repent and to have faith in Christ. What difference will it make to the way the child acts at school or with the parents? What does he or she feel about what Jesus has done? Will it mean changing the way the child prays or contributes to the life of the church? How will he react to being a representative of Christ in every situation? What will it all 'cost' that particular child, and is she prepared to give all it takes? In this way you can avoid suggesting, 'All you need to do are these five things and you will be a Christian,' which makes it seem as if Christianity is just a matter of a human's response, or, 'Just accept what God offers,' which leaves it difficult for a child to see that the step he or she is taking means anything important at all in personal terms.

## Talking about Jesus

Do positively encourage children who have a basic knowledge of the Bible to think about committing themselves to Christ. Don't be scared of doing so! Remember, however, that very young children have hardly any control over their lives at all, so to talk about an *individual* response from a child who is less than (how I hate putting a figure on it) eight is fairly meaningless. A warm exhortation to follow Christ may be all that is appropriate.

If you have been talking to an older group about what Jesus does for us today, you might say, 'If you would like to know more about what it means to be a Christian, or if you've got any questions, I'd love to talk to you about it. And if you are already a Christian, I'd love to chat to you about that as well — then we can share all the good things and difficult things that it means.' Having said this you can stand back from the situation completely and prayerfully, confident that the Holy Spirit will prompt those who are ready to take the next step in commitment to come to you. By inviting those who already have a faith in God to talk to you as well, you can allow them to deepen their commitment in any way which is appropriate, without them wondering whether they need to take the first steps all over again. It also allows those who wish to think about it for the first time to chat to you without being conscious that they are the only ones.

If you have suggested that children talk in this way, then they need to be able to do so easily. It is best to introduce an activity which children can do without close adult super-vision, freeing you to chat informally beside a child as he draws or makes a collage. Everything which makes the conversation seem 'normal' is to be encouraged. No special voice, no hushed tones, no quiet corner! There is nothing odd about becoming a Christian. It is the most natural thing that could happen to anyone, because it is what God created humans for — so don't make it seem odd by demanding special circumstances.

It is tremendously important that children are not put under emotional pressure to respond. They are acutely sensi-tive to atmosphere. It would be quite wrong to work children into a state of excitement with games and entertainments, then to appeal, with a heart-rending talk, for a mass response to Jesus. It may lead to a large number of children appearing to respond, friends in groups together, but the response may be caused by emotion alone and not be genuine. That does more damage than doing nothing. A couple of years ago, one of the teenagers in the church I belong to broke my heart by telling me, 'I've given my life to Jesus four times and it doesn't ******* work.' As we talked it became obvious that he hadn't given his life to Jesus, he had given it to the joyous and frenzied excitement of an evangelistic meeting. No wonder it didn't work! He still has a vague connection with the church and I still meet and pray for him. One day he will notice that Christianity *does* work in the quiet, unspectacular business of making your way through life as a fragile human being. Please, God.

A friend of mine, a powerful evangelist at teenage holidays, is acutely aware of the dangers of asking for a response late at night, when emotions are at their highest. He says, 'If you are genuinely interested in following Christ, I don't want to know about it now. Come and find me before breakfast tomorrow and we'll talk about it then.' And the Holy Spirit does not fail the young people, for he is not the Spirit of whim, but the Spirit of truth.

Talking to children about Jesus is a slow process. Every child is different and the conversation must be a dialogue, not a lecture. It might help, though, to have a pattern at the back of your mind so that you do not accidentally omit to talk about something important. One pattern, literal and straightforward enough for children to cope with, is based on three things which we all need to say to Jesus — thank you, sorry and please. Thank you that you came to earth because of your love for me, lived a perfect life, died and rose again. (Depending on the age of the children, you will need to explain more about the significance of all these events.) Sorry that I do wrong things, which I want to change. (Again, with older children you can begin to explain how God's actions in Jesus bring about our forgiveness.) Please let me belong to you and serve you forever. (At this point, all children need to think about the cost in human terms of serving Christ.)

It is possible, and advisable, to use a booklet geared to the right age, which you can read through together. If not, think carefully about the words you use. Stick to one expression! Do not talk about 'inviting Jesus into your life', then suddenly switch to 'being set free'. Do not begin by talking about 'being saved from your sins' and assume that children will understand that you mean the same if you then describe 'being born again'. You can find out whether children are following what you say by asking questions. Do not ask, 'Do

126

you understand that?' to which the child may simply give the answer which will please you. Instead ask, 'How do you feel about that?' and encourage reactions.

After some time you may think it is appropriate to ask, 'Do you think you would like to say a prayer asking God to accept you as one of his people?' (or whatever metaphor you have been using). Then add, 'Or would you like some more time to think about it?' The second question is important because it gives children an escape route so that they are not trapped into a move for which they are not ready. If a child says he would like more time, then accept it willingly and go on to talk with the same enthusiasm about football or U2. If he wants to go on, it would probably be helpful for you to say a prayer, quite slowly, based on the 'thank you, sorry, please' pattern. Suggest that the child says 'Amen' if he really agrees. Then tell him you're thrilled!

## The beginning, not the end

The great value of introducing children to Christ in Sunday School, rather than anywhere else, is that the leaders see children week by week and can help them grow up in the ways of God. Children who have decided to follow Jesus need continual help as they find out more, come across problems, and need to make their commitment deeper. William Temple said that, to be a Christian, a person gives 'as much as he knows of himself to as much as he knows of God'. As both areas of knowledge grow, children need more and more help to work out what it means to them to live a Christian life.

Children who have Christian families will usually have encouragement and help in continuing to serve God. It is very often a matter of great joy for Sunday School leaders to share with parents or relatives in the task of nurturing children. You might suggest to parents that they pray together with their children, and help them read the Bible regularly.

You may find yourself with slightly different responsibilities towards children whom you know will find no encouragement, or positive opposition, at home. You should not even assume that it is right for a child to tell his parents that he has made a commitment to Jesus — it might cause great stress in the family. It is best to ask children to consider, 'Would it be best to tell your family what Jesus means to you now, or try to show them something is different by the change in the way you behave?' They may need help to understand the implications of their actions, but ultimately the choice must be theirs.

It has to be said, discouraging though it is, that the proportion of children who stay faithful to Christ despite opposition or apathy at home is not large. This is not so true of adolescent teenagers, for whom turning to Christ is sometimes part of the questioning of parents' values which happens naturally at that age. However, it is a major problem for children, so churches are becoming increasingly aware that evangelism must take place in a family context, and not be directed at the child in isolation. It is very important that, if the Sunday School is taking seriously its duty to a child in its care, then the whole church (not just the Sunday School leaders) must take seriously its duty to the rest of the child's family. This might involve members of the congregation befriending the adults, inviting them to family-orientated social events, encouraging them to accompany their children to all-age family services, suggesting that they think about joining a group for those who have a slight connection with the church but are not ready yet to attend regularly, and of course, praying for them.

Ten years ago it was frequently suggested that children of non-Christian parents could be 'adopted' to find support from a family which regularly attend the church. This is still not a bad idea, but it has been overtaken by the realization that God wants to see whole families come to him as one. The idea that one could use the presence of children in the Sunday School to 'get at' their non-Christian parents now leaves a nasty taste. The good news spreads most satisfactorily by family meeting family. This is true across every potential barrier of class, race, area and family make-up. It doesn't require children to have both parents living at home, and it doesn't require them to live in a spacious house in the suburbs. It just requires friendship!

When a child is one of God's people, whether he has been so since the day he was born or whether he has only just realized the significance of what Jesus has done for him, he is your brother, or she is your sister. Sometimes brothers and sisters have good relationships, sometimes bad — but they are linked by a kinship that nothing can sever. Christian parents whose children affirm their love of Jesus, have sons and daughters who are also their brothers and sisters. Between every Sunday School leader, every child and every parent there is a family tie which demands love, respect, help, privacy at times, celebration at times, advice, encouragement, warnings and always, always an example to follow.

Now there's another thought to take your hat off to!

## Things to do

1 Make a list of all the people, events, books and experiences which have introduced you to Christ or opened up new areas of understanding for you. Which of them were formal activities that were designed for just that purpose, and which were 'accidents' in the opinion of all but the Holy Spirit?

2 Work out why you believe what you do and have put your faith in Christ. Write it down in a few sentences which are easy enough for a child to understand. Commit the sentences (or at least the gist of them) to memory.

3 Thank God for everything you have written down and pray that the children you know will grow up sharing the faith you have.

# 11 Having fun together

There has been a huge, worldwide conspiracy in churches since the Reformation which is only recently losing its grip. It says that there is something wrong with a church if people enjoy being part of it! It's not true! Of course, we must not forget that a church will be a hospital for some people at some times, and that there must be a great seriousness about the way we respond to Christ. However if, among the company of God's people, we are to live the 'life in all its fullness' that Jesus promised, it must include times of joy and fun and friendship. For children, with a smaller tolerance of boredom than adults, it is more important than ever.

From everything that has gone before it is clear that, at its most effective, Christian teaching is fun and educational simultaneously. However, there is nothing wrong with running activities from time to time which are simply for recreation. It has already become evident that a Sunday School should not only respond to children's spiritual needs. Events which help with their physical and recreational needs can be seen as part of a discipling or evangelistic programme in just as real a sense.

# Quizzes, games and competitions

These are all tremendously popular with children. Quizzes can also be useful for revision of the teaching of previous weeks, and preparation for new material. There are many ways of making them varied and exciting.

To combine a quiz with an opportunity for children to run around and lose some energy, plan a 'true or false' game. Label one end of the room 'true' and one end 'false'. Children stand in the centre and, after the leader has read out a statement, run to one end or the other. There is a temptation in this game to declare those who get it wrong 'out' and let them play no part in the rest of the quiz until a single winner survives. On the whole, I think this is unhelpful. The reasons are that you may give yourself a discipline problem if you leave a large number of children with nothing to do except watch and, more importantly, that in my experience children would rather stay in and enjoy the runaround than generate a winner and losers. To give you an idea of the sorts of statement you could make, here are a couple for you! Are these true or false (there is one of each)? 'Isaiah 37 and 2 Kings 19 are identical.' 'There are three chapters in the book of Hezekiah.' Have fun!

Alternatively, read a verse from the Bible with deliberate mistakes and ask children to spot them. For example, can you find a couple of mistakes in this extract from Matthew 2? 'Jesus was born in the town of Bethlehem in Judaea, during the time when Herod was king. Soon afterwards three kings who studied the stars came from the east to Jerusalem.'

Play a version of charades in which children act out a Bible story while others guess which one it is.

Give each child a card bearing the name of a Bible character and ask them to pair themselves. Ruth with Boaz, Ananias with Sapphira, and so on.

All kinds of methods of scoring can be based on television programmes, such as *Blockbusters*, or children's games, such as *Connect 4*. Those will go out of date quickly, but score charts in which rockets fly to Mars or newspaper trees grow are timeless.

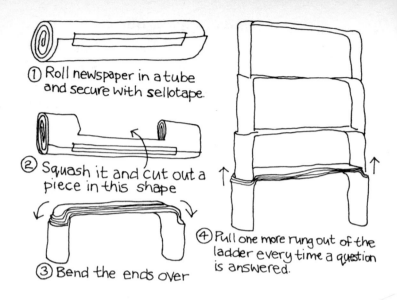

1. Roll newspaper in a tube and secure with sellotape.

2. Squash it and cut out a piece in this shape

3. Bend the ends over

4. Pull one more rung out of the ladder every time a question is answered.

## Are quizzes always good?

I am hesitant to answer 'yes', because quizzes which are presented thoughtlessly can hurt. It is always right to ask yourself whether your quiz is fair, particularly since children have such a strongly developed sense of justice. Is the quiz fair to children who have not got a great deal of biblical knowledge because they do not happen to have parents who are interested in the Bible? Is it fair to children with academic difficulties, who may feel a sense of failure? A quiz which is just a glory ride for bright kids is doing no one any good. It may help in these circumstances to score by throwing dice — that way the quiz is useful revision and good fun, but the score does not make cleverness the sole virtue.

I am also slightly concerned about groups which consistently have quizzes which are challenge matches between the girls and the boys. Since one of the features of Christianity we want to teach is that men and women are entirely equal in God's sight, it would seriously undermine our teaching if the girls were consistently egged on to prove themselves better than the boys and *vice versa*. Obviously that does not rule out the occasional boys *v.* girls game, but it would be unhelpful if that were the only form of competition on offer in church.

Some people would go further and suggest that any kind of competitive game in a church is likely to counteract the gospel principle that we do not have to be better or stronger or more religious than anyone else in order to be accepted by God. They would suggest that instead we offer the children cooperative games, in which a challenge is set and the children have to work together in order to fulfil the objective successfully. This is a much more realistic model of what the Christian life is to be like than a constant desire to beat the other team down. An example of a cooperative game is the very enjoyable one in which the children or adults stand in a huddle and reach across the group to take another hand in each hand. By working together, stepping over, twisting around and winding underneath each other, they must untangle themselves into one unbroken circle. Success generates a great deal of satisfaction and everyone ends up feeling good about themselves.

As one who has consistently been beaten at tennis by my godson ever since he was barely as tall as the net, I would be sorry to be deprived of the opportunity to lose gracefully at competitive games! On the other hand, I can sympathize with the child who, from Monday to Friday, is made to feel a failure again and again when he or she is the last to be picked for teams at school, comes bottom of the class in spelling tests and feels humiliated by Sports Day when losing is a very public affair. Wouldn't it be good if children like that could look on Sunday School as the only place in their world where they can go in confidence that they will never be made to feel inferior to others? It would be a valuable lesson about how God views life's priorities in a totally different way from most of the world's population. It is worth considering whether Sunday School can provide a regular alternative to competition, not just for the sake of what it does to the losers, but for the sake of what it does to the winners!

# Midweek activities

It can be of great benefit to a group which meets on a Sunday if that meeting is periodically supplemented by an activity on a weekday evening or a Saturday. Very often leaders and children can form better relationships on a Sunday because of the fun they share at a less formal 'club' during the week.

These club events can consist of games, hobbies and craft groups, long-term projects, serial stories, and they can also have some biblical content in the form of revision of what is done on a Sunday or extension of it to cover more ground. If the activities can be related to the main theme of the week, for example, making a cassette tape to send to a missionary family after teaching on overseas mission, or cooking unleavened bread after teaching on the Passover, so much the better.

As well as helping the children to develop their relationships, an event such as this may be an easier introduction to church life than the main meeting for a child who has no previous experience of attending a Sunday School.

# Outings

Outings are also very beneficial to the way groups are built into a community and learn how Christians should treat each other. There is something to be said for traditions of revisiting the same place and something to be said for variety. The children are in the best possible position to tell you where they would like to go. They rarely get asked, but it would be good for them to learn about making decisions democratically and taking responsibility for giving themselves a good time, rather than expecting it to happen automatically.

I have only one piece of advice, and I learnt that the hard way. Make sure that the adult to child ratio is good enough to mean that there is absolutely no chance of a child going astray. I once lost a boy among a crowd of sixty thousand at a hot-air balloon festival. My worries were greatly multiplied by the fact that I had earlier seen a man talking to him about the scout T-shirt he was wearing. As it happened, the incident was innocuous and the boy turned up, red-eyed and

*'Up, up and away!'*

frightened, an hour later, having sensibly latched himself on to a colleague's group. In my relief, I found myself apologizing for losing him, rather than telling him off for wandering away. He won't get away so lightly next time — but then there won't be a next time!

There are a few rules of thumb which help prevent this happening. Make sure that each adult is personally responsible for a specific group of children and can recognize the names and faces of those in his or her care. Tell children in advance precisely what to do and where to go if they get lost — make sure everyone is listening at that stage, which may be more difficult than it sounds if the children are in a state of excitement. Tell them also what you want them to do if a stranger approaches them, but not in a way which leaves them terrified of any adult who is simply friendly towards children by nature. Given those precautions, you can rely on the fact that children, on the whole, don't want to get lost, and motorists, on the whole, don't want to knock children down, to prevent you ruining your day with worry.

# Parties

As with outings, it is the children themselves who are likely to give you the best advice as to what to do at a party. It is probably better to err on the side of sophistication, rather than childishness — but if the event is well-organized and fast-moving, and the leader can create enthusiasm, children can be won over to anything that has a high fun factor.

If you are aiming at building relationships through a party, then the activities which you offer need to involve children and leaders communicating. An evening in the cinema probably won't achieve this, but a ten pin bowling or crazy golf afternoon might. A 'theme' party, where children come in fancy dress and the games are adapted to fit the theme, can give a sense of unity to a group. The subject could be 'Invasion of the Aliens from Space', 'Scarecrows Alive!' or 'Pirates Ahoy!' Beware the temptation of feeling that activities such as this must have a Christian flavour to them — simply naming the teams 'Matthew, Mark, Luke and John' does not turn a relay race into a religious event! For a spectacular event that requires minimum effort, hire an inflatable and let the children bounce themselves into exhaustion. It will cost less than you imagine. The council youth department will probably be able to tell you where you can get one.

Parties are great opportunities to let generations mix. It's valuable for all churches to hold social events which express the all-age nature of the Christian faith. It becomes even more important if the children do not regularly see Christian adults apart from their own leaders. To watch grown-up Christians enjoying themselves is a useful role model for children in a society where a great deal of adult entertainment involves excess of one kind or another. These need not be events for families only — they can answer a real need for single people who miss the opportunity to enjoy children's company. Try going swimming together or having a picnic followed by games. A barn dance can be enjoyed by many generations at the same time. So can a drama workshop, a craft afternoon or a nostalgia evening, when everyone shares memories of their first teachers, the toys they used to play with, their happiest and most embarrassing moments, and so on. It may be easier to invite parents who do not accompany their children to church to this kind of event rather than to a service, as an introduction to the fellowship.

## Things to do

**1** Look at the list which follows. Note down five items or names in each category. (Remember that they must be suitable for sevens to elevens.) If you need to borrow books from the library to help you, look at your diary now to plan when you will go.

(a) Methods of scoring a quiz.
(b) Indoor games.
(c) Outdoor games.
(d) Places near enough to visit on an outing.
(e) Social events that adults and children can attend together.
(f) Members of the church with an interesting hobby which they could teach or demonstrate.
(g) Films available on video.
(h) Books which could be serialized to read aloud.
(i) Themes for a party.

**2** Copy your lists on to file cards and put them in an accessible place. On each card, write down the equipment you need to operate the event. Add to the file every time you see or hear about someone else's bright idea.

# 12

# Sugar and spice v. slugs and snails

I was once showing two new infants around the junior section of the school in which I was teaching. I had one in each hand and was chatting to them about how strict the junior teachers were and how important it was to do just what they were told immediately. Suddenly I saw one of my own class running at full tilt down the corridor. Frightened that he would damage either himself or the school, I shouted at the top of my voice, 'Neil!' . . . and the two infants knelt down! I've been frightened of my own power ever since!

There have been occasions in Sunday School when I wished I had one tenth of the control that I had unexpectedly over those infants. I remember the day I discovered that one of my boys (I won't tell you his name, it wouldn't be fair) had poured white spirit over the plants we had been growing and killed them stone dead. That night I had a disturbing, but oddly satisfying, dream in which I was preaching to rank upon rank of children, gagged into silence and tied helplessly to their seats. I shall also never forget the day I went berserk in front of a thirteen-year-old girl who had found balloons hidden in the corners of the church hall and, even though it must have been obvious that I had put them there as part of a game for the five-year-olds, had taken a safety pin and burst the lot. I was so remorseful afterwards that I had to spend a long time sorting myself out with God before I could apologize to her.

Most of the time, though, my problems have not been as dramatic as that. When I feel control slipping away from me, it is usually because someone is making a noise when I need attention, or disturbing another child by making him uncomfortable, or making foolish comments and actions when the activity calls for seriousness. The boy with the white spirit has behavioural problems which it is taking more than a Sunday School to solve, but Lucy rubbed *Plasticine* into Gareth's hair the week before last because she was bored!

The old nursery rhyme tells us that boys are made of slugs and snails and puppy-dog's tails, but that girls are made of sugar and spice and all things nice. However, in my experience all those splendid and nasty things exist inside all children! And because children do not put church in a separate compartment, there is no reason why either boys or girls should bring only their 'sugar and spice' nature to the Sunday School. Most children simply react to what is going on in the best way they know — and there is nothing like boredom to bring the slugs and snails out of the hedgerow!

There is no secret formula for discipline, but there is a long, laborious process of building up relationships of trust and care, so that there is no cause for children to be disobedient. Their natural instinct is to love adults, not to annoy them — to want to enjoy themselves, not to disrupt.

## Keeping control

If children are consistently getting out of control, there are some questions that need to be asked about your programme, and some to ask about the children.

Are the children bored because the subject is being presented in a way which seems to have no relevance to their lives? This may be a particular problem among early teenage

139

children who are beginning to ask searching questions about life. It can be a genuine embarrassment to appear to be listening to something 'two thousand years out of date' when your friends are only interested in today. The first thing a leader with this difficulty ought to do is examine how much of the programme is taken up with an adult declaiming and how much allows children to give their own hot-off-the-press opinions. If you genuinely believe that Jesus' claims are relevant to today's society, there is no need to be scared of discussing at length the world the children live in.

Are you using language and ideas which are correctly geared to the age of the children? I'm not sure which is more likely to bring trouble — being naive and babyish with older children, or being too complicated for young children. In both cases, the problem is magnified when hymns and prayers are either laughably infantile or too long and full of religious words. Of course, the length of any individual item needs to be geared properly too — young children need a lot more variety because they simply cannot concentrate for so long.

Is there too much passive listening? Children who are doing something interesting with their own hands, eyes and ears are less likely to be disruptive. I have always worked on the principle that listening involves only one of the children's senses — that leaves four senses and an awful lot of energy to be used, either to create and discover and learn, or to make trouble!

Has a child got difficulties outside the Sunday School which affect his or her behaviour inside it? This is a different sort of question from the last three, and needs a different response. Many factors may be involved. A child may consistently be ignored or put down in school and find the only way to get attention is to play up. Another may be unhappy because quarrels and crises at home have made her insecure. Resentment at being sent to Sunday School when the alternative is being in a football team could also be a problem. All of these need an individual approach and will involve talking to others, especially parents if that is possible. Pastoral problems like these are a long time in the solving — and the leader's role may simply be to pray and be as supportive as possible. In these situations, you must be careful not to blame yourself, but also not to add to the child's problems by making Sunday School oppressive.

## Emergency action

Even with a programme chock-full of excitement and an overflowing love for children, every leader is going to be faced with situations in which he needs to act quickly. The long term solutions suggested above don't help at the precise moment when Paul drops his extremely realistic, rubber spider down Amanda's dress. So here is some on-the-spot action which you can take.

Use a voice that is sharp enough to show that you expect to be obeyed, but don't shout. You have had authority given to you, so don't be afraid to use it. There is no need to worry that this will make you unpopular — respect and popularity often go hand in hand. Obviously, only respect earns respect, and it is important to remember to be courteous. It is just as necessary to say 'please' and 'thank you' to children as it is to adults. The real test is whether you have enough respect to say 'sorry' to a child when the situation demands it.

If you are interrupted while you are talking, stand firm and wait for silence before you carry on. Look determined! However, if you sense that the group has completely lost interest in what you are saying, get them doing something active *straight away*. Sarcastic comments won't get you anywhere!

Have a few consistent rules and make sure the children know what they are. Be careful that the standard you expect stays the same from week to week, and does not vary between one child and another. When the rules are clear, enforce them rather than giving repeated warnings (If you say, 'I won't tell you again,' twice, the ill-disciplined child has won!) In the same way, don't make threats which you do not intend to fulfil. To my shame, I remember once telling a girl, 'If you don't stop kicking Gavin, I'll make sure you never kick anything again.' I can't imagine what came over me — the comment did nobody any good at all!

If you are having trouble with a particular child, ask him or her to sit in a different place, away from the distraction. If there is a chance of the incident recurring, make the offender sit next to you and give him or her something specific to do. This will not only occupy the child in a more constructive way, but will provide a chance for you to give praise later on for a task done well. Repeated congratulations for positive behaviour help to reduce a child's need to gain attention with wayward behaviour.

If you really can't cope, don't be afraid to send a child out of the room. Of course, you need to be absolutely sure that you are not putting anyone's safety or security at risk by doing this. After a couple of minutes, a leader can go out and calmly explain what went wrong. Be certain to have an interesting activity for the child to come back to as soon as possible — the risk is that outside will prove more appealing and there will be a repeat!

## Is it just a matter of survival?

Obviously you need to be able to keep reasonable control of the children in your care for you own peace of mind. But that is not the most important reason. For children, learning to be disciplined is part of learning to be a disciple. 'Jesus went back with his parents to Nazareth,' we are told, 'where he was obedient to them . . . he grew both in body and in wisdom, gaining favour with God and men' (Luke 2:51–52). God's desire for Christian children is for them to emulate Jesus when he was a child at the same stage of development. Self-control, consideration of others, hard work — all these may well be part of the obedience that God calls for. He is a God of righteousness, as well as a God of love, and an 'anything-goes' Sunday School may give children the mistaken impression that we have an anything-goes God.

But our gracious God cares for you just as much as he cares for the children. He doesn't want you to be upset week after week if things are going wrong. He is never going to label you as a failure if the group is proving more than you can handle! He understands!

If you have got tough kids in your group, start off by thanking God that he has motivated them to come at all. Then tell him exactly what you feel about the situation — if you secretly wish the awkward ones would go away, then be honest with him, but be prepared for him to show you that they need the good news about Jesus just as much as the children you like a lot. Thirdly, and very importantly, talk about it to others in your church, not afraid that they will think you have failed, but expecting them to share your frustrations and support you. Fourthly, fill the kettle, switch on the TV and think about something else until it is time to prepare for next week!

## Things to do

**1** Write down what you consider to be the 'rules' of your Sunday School. Do the children know them? Are there too many? What do you plan to do if a child breaks one? Are they asking the impossible of children?

**2** What have you observed to be the points in your programme at which children are most likely to misbehave? What activities have you noticed children getting so absorbed in that there are few discipline problems? Have you got the proportions right between the former and the latter?

**3** Do just what the last paragraph of the chapter suggests!

# 13

# How to keep children out of church

Start by making it consistently the least interesting thing they do all week. Only talk about Christianity in terms of what happened two thousand years ago, so that they do not suspect it has any relevance to life today. Never let them see the adult section of the church in action until, in their mid or early teens, you push them out of the top end of Sunday School and tell them to do the best they can in the 'real' church. Under no circumstances invite or listen to their opinions about any of these things. That should effectively prevent children becoming adult church members — and with real devotion to the task, the church can be closed down in, say, ten years!

Please, God, no!

## Children and adults in church

If all that has been said about young Christians needing adults and adult Christians needing children is true, then there should be occasions when they approach God side by side. It's not an optional extra. It is the life-blood of a growing and ongoing church.

The 1988 report for the Church of England's General Synod, *Children in the Way*, so beautifully pictures the way a church can offer a 'pilgrimage' model for children and adults, that it is worth reproducing in full.

'Imagine a group of people of all ages going on a long walk together. At times the children and adults will walk along together, talking as they go, sharing stories with first one person and then another, each observing different things and sharing their discoveries. At times the children will lag behind and the adults will have to wait for them and urge them on. Sometimes the smallest children may ask to be carried. At other times, though, the children will dash ahead making new discoveries and may, perhaps, pull the adults along to see what they have found. Some adults may well behave like these children, of course. For all there will be times of progress and times of rest and refreshment, time to admire the view, and times of plodding on, and the eventual satisfaction of arrival at their destination.

'Of course, a pilgrimage is something more than a hike. Traditionally it is a group of people of all kinds and ages united in reaching a common goal. They stop at significant places on the way. They exchange their own stories, and share past experiences and memories of those who have gone before them. They look forward to the rest of the journey and to reaching their ultimate destination.' (General Synod Board of Education, Church House Publishing.)

## Parents and children

With a few disturbing exceptions, children of the ages covered by this book live with adults — given a loose enough definition of the word, they live in families. Attention has already been drawn to the emphasis the Bible puts on the responsibility of parents, and those in the position of parents, to bring up their own children to know and love God. The references go on and on. 'Be on your guard! Make certain that you do not forget, as long as you live, what you have

145

seen with your own eyes. Tell your children and your grandchildren ... I want them to hear what I have to say, so that they will learn to obey me as long as they live and so that they will teach their children to do the same' (Deuteronomy 4:9–10).

Even if the Bible were not so frank, simple mathematics would be convincing. In an average week, children spend about one hour in Sunday School, and a mere hundred and twelve times that in their homes. A typical week might be divided like this:

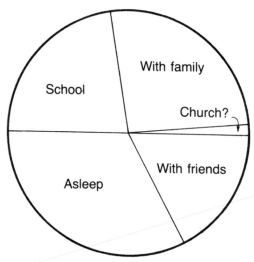

Children do not reserve their important questions for the specified hour when church meets — and they certainly cannot wait for their answers until then. The answers must make sense in the context of what they experience elsewhere in home life if they are to ring true.

Churches can provide parents with help and support in bringing up their families. They can provide workshops and seminars on family-related issues. They can equip parents with information and resources. Members of a congregation can fill family gaps when aunts, uncles, godparents or grandparents live far away. In these circumstances, the wisdom of older people who have accumulated experience of life is a

146

huge asset. The church can offer times of celebration for whole families and put families together to share, care for and advise each other.

To organize all these sources of help is not the responsibility of a Sunday School leader — he or she has enough of a load to bear already. However, if the work of a Sunday School is done in the context of sustained help for parents as they nurture their children, its impact must be greatly enhanced.

## All-age services

These are regular services, usually monthly, sometimes quarterly, at which the entire congregation spends the whole session together, taking part in praise, teaching and prayer. They are sometimes known as 'family services', which is a good title if the congregation realizes that it refers to the entire church as a family, but a bad title if single people and those whose children have grown up infer that they will not find them relevant.

An important feature of all-age services is that adults must not find them simply childish, and that children must not find that adults have made no concessions at all to the fact that they are present. This means that the hymns and prayers need not aim at the lowest common denominator, but should be carefully prepared so that most of the words are accessible to most of the people present most of the time.

Hymns which have simple refrains are particularly useful for children who, even if they can actually read the words in a hymn book, may only be able to grasp one idea from each song. Prayers for the sick, for current affairs and for church events can be understood by children and adults at once — although it is helpful if they are shorter than they might usually be. One possibility is to ask a family from the congregation to lead them — both children and adults reading prayers that they have previously prepared. A great deal of what was said in chapter 7 about worship with children is relevant to adults as well, did they but know it, and could be applied to an all-age service.

147

The sermon or talk will almost certainly require visual aids. It need not even be recognizable as a traditional sermon — it could be split into two or three short statements, given at different points in the service. Like a children's talk, it will require anecdotes and examples, as well as explanation of a Bible passage. It is helpful if each point made has an illustrative example at the children's level, and then one at the adults' level, so that no one feels that the truth is irrelevant to them. A good technique is to ask the congregation to form themselves into groups of three or four, by turning on their seats, to discuss a question. It should be an open-ended question which has many possible answers at child-level and at adult-level. For example, during teaching on the need for Christians to witness to others about their faith, groups could be asked to help create a list of the practical ways of doing this that are appropriate to the children and adults present. After a couple of minutes talking together (or thinking by themselves, which should be offered as an alternative), they can be asked to call out their suggestions. The speaker can comment on the thoughts that all have contributed as he or she writes them on a chart or overhead projector.

It need hardly be said that, if children are comfortable with the idea of taking part in a service in the main building of the church, it will reduce the possibility of tension when they grow to the age at which they are expected, at some point in their teens, to stay in the adult section of the church full-time.

148

# Together every week

A growing pattern in churches is for all ages to spend a part of every service, perhaps ten to twenty minutes, together. During this time, the congregation sings, prays, praises God, watches a drama, hears a Bible reading, states a creed, enjoys a revision quiz, hears a testimony or does any one of a hundred other activities which glorify or teach about God.

This can come at the beginning of a service, which allows a family to approach the worship of God as a unit, but makes it quite difficult for a child whose parents have no connection with the church to come for the first time. It can also come at the end of a service, which is particularly valuable if adults and children have both been following one syllabus and can all respond in worship to the same newly-learnt truths. Both bring with them the problem of a brief disruption to the service as children enter or leave, but there are local solutions which most churches should be able to work out with a little imagination and sensitivity.

It is particularly valuable for children to be present periodically, if not weekly, at the administration of communion. In some churches this will mean receiving the elements, and in others receiving a blessing. Both of these are good preparations for and encouragements to adult membership of a church, for they unite the entire congregation in the act of remembrance which Jesus gave us for that very reason.

# Could a child be a leader?

A service is an event to which we go to serve. That's how it gets its name! There is no reason why children should not be offered a chance to serve God and serve one another on a regular basis — and in some cases that may involve leading certain events. Children can be asked to prepare a prayer, to read a poem or Bible passage, to take part in a drama designed to make the congregation think. They can help to give out hymn books, to serve coffee, to stack chairs or to collect an offertory. They can be asked in advance to choose hymns, to accompany them on recorders, guitars or

149

percussion, or to prepare visual aids for the speaker to use as part of a talk.

This not only helps children to appropriate the church as their own, it also teaches them that it is their business to give their efforts to God, not merely to take the enjoyment that the church offers them. As a bonus, it is usually true that involving children in this way is a happy experience both for the children and the adults. ('Aaah! Aren't the little ones sweet!')

## There are other ways of learning

Some valuable ways of learning simply do not fit into the format of a congregational service, and it would be sad if a church missed out on them because its traditions restricted it to Sunday worship.

In some churches, groups of adults meet together on a Saturday or a public holiday to explore a theme more fully than is possible on a Sunday. They make banners, play games which have a meaning, devise drama, cook food, record tapes, practise new songs, shoot videos, share their experiences — and sometimes their work is incorporated in a Sunday service on another occasion. The event may include Bible study and prayer, but it also offers creative experiences which open up new learning possibilities.

An all-age group can, for example, work together on a collage called 'Who is my neighbour?' The first value is the satisfaction of learning to work together and complete a project for others to see. It allows all to learn about cooperation, agreeing together, being sensitive to others' needs, and many features of the Christian life about which adults need to discover as much as children. The second value is that, as the artists talk and decide together what form the collage should take, they find out about each others' lives, the neighbourhoods in which they live, the stresses of life in parts of the area about which they know little, and so on. Adults can learn how tough it is to be a Christian 'neighbour' at school — which may astound and challenge them. Children can be encouraged by the practical difference God made to the way an older generation served the neighbourhood during the war. When they later hear the story of the good Samaritan, which Jesus told in response to the question, 'Who is my neighbour?', they will understand it in the context of the real experiences of other Christian people — and their completed collage will be a long-term reminder.

There are a number of resource books available for those who need help or reliable ideas for projects such as these. The best training, though, is to invite yourself to a similar event which someone else is running in a nearby church and learn by enjoying it alongside them.

To use all these methods is categorically not a guarantee that children will grow into mature Christian members of a congregation. That is the work of the Holy Spirit, and it must be our prayer that we do everything to help and nothing to hinder him. However, to make churches the very reverse of the one featured in the first paragraph of the chapter — interesting, integrated, creative, up-to-date, meeting needs, relevant and involving, even at the youngest age — is to teach things about God at heart-level, not merely at head-level. And what a child learns about God deep in his or her spirit is not readily given away.

## Things to do

1  Look back at the four models for children's involvement in church life which were given at the beginning of chapter 4. Which does your own church most resemble? What are the strengths of that approach to children's work? What are the weaknesses?

2  What could the children in your group offer as a way of serving the whole church? Re-read the list in the section of this chapter titled 'Could a child be a leader?' Underline any suggestion that you could, without causing distress to large numbers of adult members, envisage children doing periodically as a part of their service. With whom would you have to broach the matter?

3  Most of the issues talked about in this chapter are out of

the control of individual Sunday School leaders. If you have been struck by any frustrations over what you would like to see in your church, but are powerless to change, make a written note of them. Begin to pray for opportunities to share your ideas in a sensitive way with those who make decisions in the church.

# 14

# Leaders... and other problems

Let's eavesdrop on a conversation after an infuriating hour in a Sunday School!

'I just can't stand leading the group anymore.'

'You've had a hard morning! I sympathize.'

'It's astonishing how one person can disrupt a whole Sunday School.'

'It's a discipline problem, is it?'

'Yes! I just can't handle him. He stops all the others enjoying themselves. Nothing I do to make Sunday School enjoyable seems to satisfy him. Children are leaving. Parents wonder why I can't control him. I feel like giving up.'

'You can't let a single ten-year-old get you down like this.'

'Ten-year-old? I'm talking about the minister!'

## What's required in a good leader?

I think the conversation I just made up hit below the belt. There must be very few churches where those criticisms would be fair. Nevertheless, it is certainly true that there are Sunday Schools everywhere in which the relationships

153

between the leaders are not all that they could be. To find out what makes for good teamwork, let's go right back to basics!

## Absolute essentials

There are some qualifications without which a Sunday School leader should not even be considered.

### A leader should be a Christian

When I was teaching disco dance at school I used to go to an evening class on Wednesday, master a couple of new steps, then pass on what I had learnt to my school class on Friday. But the Sunday School leader is not a teacher mugging up a Bible story and telling it for what it's worth. He is in the business of allowing God to change lives. She is about the work of new creation. It would be rare for a leader to enable a child to make a relationship with Jesus Christ which the leader does not share.

In most cases, an adult Christian would not make himself or herself available for Sunday School leadership unless it sprang from a commitment to serving God. There is, however, a seductive temptation to try to cling on to barely committed teenagers who are losing interest in church attendance by involving them in the Sunday School. Hard and fast rules cannot be laid down in these circumstances — they need delicate pastoral handling. However, it is worth noting that, for the sake of the Sunday School children and for the sake of the teenager, this easy option may not be the wisest. There is too much at stake to take risks.

### A leader should have an elementary Bible knowledge

That is not to say that every leader needs to be a theological expert before he begins. However, there are some basic facts about Jesus' life, the Bible, and the way the Holy Spirit lives in Christians which set the context for all we try to do in Sunday School. They are facts that any daily Bible-reading scheme or structured system of preaching will cover regularly, because every Christian should know them. It is probably advizable that a brand new Christian, even though he or she may be bursting with enthusiasm for children's work, should spend a little time learning before passing on what has been discovered.

## A leader needs to be fond of children
It is true that God will 'equip you with everything good for doing his will' (Hebrews 13:21), but it is not his will for everyone without exception to hit it off with children. 'Each one', we are told in 1 Peter 4:10, 'should use whatever gift he has received to serve others.' If you simply do not enjoy children's company, then it is worth asking yourself whether Sunday School leadership really is the gift that the Holy Spirit has given you. If it is not, then there is no reason to feel guilty about turning down the offer of a place on the team and seeking to serve God in some other area of church life.

## Leaders should be praying people
Those who are not in contact with God, in whatever form they find appropriate, have switched off the power supply that makes a Sunday School work.

# Qualities that leaders should show

The four essentials listed above would apply even if a leader was working by himself with the children. Working in a team has great advantages, but successful team work does not happen by accident. My job description for a team member would additionally feature a list of demanding adjectives!

### Reliable
Leaders need to know that they can rely on each other to be there when they have said they will (barring illness or accidents, of course), to be on time, and to be prepared.

In my experience, it helps for all the leaders to agree on what their commitment to the Sunday School group is. There can be no possible confusion if each leader has a piece of paper on which are written the times and days of the children's activities they are to attend, the number of minutes early they will arrive to set up equipment, the amount of time that they should expect to spend per week in personal preparation, the frequency of leaders' meetings, any expectation of them to visit children in their homes or help with outings and parties, even the number of years or terms they foresee themselves serving. The list could also include things that leaders are specifically not required to do — for instance, giving a sermon at an all-age service — if they need reassurance that they will not be stretched beyond the limit of their gifts.

I once got myself into a difficult position when a young leader, about whom I knew little when I welcomed her on to the team, proved unsuitable for the task she had taken on. She was an A-level student and had not registered that she would be required to do some planning and preparation, as well as attending the group on a Sunday morning. She simply hadn't got time to manage it. I got no pleasure at all from explaining to her that I thought she and I had both made a mistake. Ever since then I have discussed with new leaders exactly what is needed and asked them to sign an agreement as to how much and how little they can commit themselves to — a sort of informal contract. The lady in question went on to give excellent service to God in the drama group — you knew that story would have a happy ending, didn't you!

## Loyal

As a leader, you lose certain rights! One is the right to take a Sunday off on whim. Another is the right to criticize other leaders of the church behind their backs. In some cases this means fighting against great frustration. It includes resisting the temptation to join an 'our-minister-has-got-it-all-wrong' caucus. And that still applies if the minister makes life very difficult for the Sunday School. Yes, I mean it!

That is not to say leaders should silently put up with all kinds of unhelpful attitudes and wrong actions from their fellow leaders. The Christian way to deal with these problems is to approach the person who is causing the difficulty, lovingly, privately and after prayer. As part of his instruction on how to serve Jesus as his 'body', the church, Paul advises us that 'by speaking the truth in a spirit of love, we must grow up in every way to Christ, who is the head' (Ephesians

4:15). It is a question of motive. If we have in mind the genuine desire to improve the way the whole church (not just the Sunday School) serves God, then we can take courage to suggest that a person changes the attitude which is causing a problem. However, there is no permission given in the Bible to work a moan out of your system by gossiping about someone. It helps no one.

Part of our loyalty to other leaders is to give encouragement. It takes hardly any effort at all to congratulate someone when they tell a story well, or sort out the problems of a crying child, or invent an enjoyable game. Yet it makes a vast difference — not because it is flattering, but because it reassures people that they have selected a good approach and gives them courage to try something similar, or potentially even better, in future. Encouragement actually improves the quality of what happens in church.

Conversely, a person who does something less than well sometimes needs help in order to do it better next time. As a trainee teacher in an infant school, I had the bright idea of making collages of Humpty Dumpty from pieces of broken eggshell. It was a catastrophe! The eggshells were too thin and crumbled to dust, the paste was watery, and ran into the children's nails and hair, they lost interest through sheer frustration, and one of them twirled himself round and round inside the window curtains and refused to come out. It was the nearest I got to giving up teaching forever.

My rescue came in the form of the teacher who was supervising me. To my shame, I can't remember her name, but she had thick brown stockings and a quiet voice which could, at will, surge into a brontosaural bellow. If you recognize yourself from that description, then thank you, because you did precisely what I needed you to do. You didn't tell me what I could already see with my own eyes — that I had made a complete hippo's breakfast of that activity. Instead, you quietly and cheerfully sent the children into the playground, grabbed a broom, and helped me sort through the debris. Then you fetched me a coffee and told me about the disastrous lessons for which you had been responsible in the past. We laughed until my drink was slopping all over the saucer. You said no more about it until a week later when I was preparing for another craft lesson. By then I had cooled off and was in a far better position to take your very positive advice on how to organize the activity so that the same mishaps did not take place again. Everything you said was wise and, better still, it was wisely timed. Wherever you are, you have my undying gratitude, and I hope the ingrowing toenail has stopped giving you jip!

## Cooperative

Directors always tell actors that it is not only when they are speaking their own lines that they are important — all the time they are on stage, their reactions and expressions contribute to the impact made on the audience. The same is true in children's work. When not leading an activity, leaders should sit among the children, showing their interest in what is going on. If you fix your gaze on the colleague who is running a quiz or giving a testimony, your interest is infectious. If you look as though your thoughts are distracted or, worse still, if you chat to your fellow-workers, the children will do so too. It will help to maintain discipline if, without making it obvious, leaders identify in advance the places where trouble might develop, and sit close to those.

Part of being cooperative is the willingness to pray regularly for those alongside whom you work. Don't just pray for the work they do in the children's group, but for all their lives and families. Praying for people involves knowing their needs and being prepared to help in some circumstances.

One aspect of cooperation which requires self-discipline is to look objectively at your own part in the team and ask whether you are creating unnecessary obstacles. Knowing when to retire is a problem for some, and to be able to do so without either allowing the group to collapse or outstaying your usefulness requires wisdom and a gracious spirit. I guess that when you start to say, 'I don't seem to understand the children's world as well as I used to,' it is way past the time when you should have been thinking about training a new leader to take your place. On the day when I say, 'Kids don't change — my method worked twenty years ago and it will work today,' I hope someone will tap me on the shoulder and point to this paragraph. I shall ask God towards which different area of Christian service he is leading me.

## Making a team work

All the suggestions that have gone before rely on individuals contributing to the well-being of a team. However, there are some features of teamwork which require organization.

If a children's group meets weekly, then its leaders ought to meet monthly to plan. If they meet less often than that, decisions can be delayed unhelpfully. If they meet more often, it puts unfair demands on an individual's time. Evenings with friends and family, other church activities, housework, and time spent living out the faith among non-Christians are all important too.

At a leaders' meeting it is useful to review everything that has happened over the past month. If something needs changing, it is easier to do it as part of a regular reordering than to wait until it leads to a crisis. The joys and problems of particular children should be discussed, successes or failures of the programme should be noted.

Detailed planning for the coming month should follow, with all the leaders taking notes, or being given them subsequently, so that there is a written record of what each leader is to do on particular dates in the future.

Last in this list, but not necessarily in the meeting, should be specific prayer about the decisions which have been made and for individual children.

It would do the team no harm to meet together very occasionally just for fun — a meal or a cup of tea. That, however, is meant to bring pleasure, not to be an added pressure in a crowded diary.

## Coordination

If the youth work of a church is fragmented into different age-groups, it is important for information to be passed between them. This can either take place at a wider meeting of leaders or by the appointment of a coordinator whose

159

specific task it is to keep children's groups and the leaders whose primary responsibility is the adult section of the church in touch with each other.

The time when this is most significant is when children progress from one age-group to another. It is not by any means an easy change for children to make, but there are some ways of making the move less traumatic. One is to allow the oldest children to visit their next group for ten minutes or so on three or four occasions before the day they make the move permanently. They should be accompanied to the new room or new section of the room by a leader with whom they are familiar, and introduced personally to the leaders of their future group. It is usually right that children should be moved to new groups as a pastoral decision, not strictly on the basis of age. It would, for example, be unwise to split up close friends of a similar age simply because their birthdays fall on either side of a particular date. To move groups of children on a termly, rather than yearly, basis prevents dramatic increases or reductions in the numbers of children in each group and makes the change-dates loom less dauntingly. There are, however, no hard and fast rules on this — the important factor is that everyone should agree on a single policy.

## Training

It is impossible to underestimate the value of training, not because of the instruction an expert gives, but because the shared experience of those who work in the same field is both challenging and encouraging. It can be arranged informally within a church, with an honest and experienced colleague watching you in action, helping you to reflect on what you do well and how you could improve in other areas. There is also virtue in spending a day or weekend with members of other churches, whose different perspectives and ideas can unlock skills inside you to the benefit of the children and the enrichment of the church. If you use a published Sunday School syllabus, it will almost certainly have a training scheme or pack associated with it. Reading this book has already begun your training. Using the questions at the end of each chapter for discussion with other leaders would be a valuable step forward. Working and sharing with other Christians for the rest of your life will continue the process until, in Heaven, we all get to be experts!

## Keeping the congregation informed

The task of bringing up children to know Christ is not just the job of the Sunday School leaders — it is the responsibility of the whole congregation. Keep the church leadership team constantly informed about the state of the Sunday School — it is, after all, they who are ultimately accountable for the children. A gentle and loving reminder of this would not be inappropriate for a minister who seems not to care for the children's groups. Keep the rest of the congregation informed, too, of times when new leaders are needed, of particular causes for rejoicing, of the problems you are trying to overcome because the premises are not suitable or the numbers are too high or too low. If the church has a news sheet, use it to give Sunday School information. If notices are announced, make your needs public that way. If intercessions are made as part of the service, regularly request prayer for specific things. It would not, of course, be right to use these means to criticize covertly those who are failing to support you — but to remind the entire congregation that anything up to a third of their number are elsewhere while they are enjoying their sermon is not a criticism, it is a lifeline!

## Compensation

Those not directly involved sometimes forget that most Sunday School leaders miss out on regular Bible teaching and the fellowship of meeting and worshipping with the congregation because of their commitment to the children. Some kind of compensation is needed so that they do not lose touch with the encouragements of the faith that others take for granted.

One possibility is to make it a condition of leadership that leaders attend an evening service. It can mean not only that the leaders retain fellowship with the adult congregation, but also that the energy of the evening service is transformed, prompting others to attend as well. In some churches there is no evening service, so the minister meets with the leaders once a week to study the passage that the children will be exploring later. This is, of course, time-consuming and everyone involved needs to think very carefully before committing themselves to another meeting per week.

A less satisfactory solution is a rota. Experience keeps reminding me that it is the quality of the relationships we form with children that ultimately teaches them most about the Kingdom of God. A leader who sees the children for an hour or so once a month can fill them with facts about Christ, but cannot really care for pastoral needs, win their affection and grow in his relationship with individual children. If a rota is unavoidable, it should be under the supervision of an overall leader who stays with the children week in, week out. In a tiny fellowship, where everyone knows each other very well, this becomes less important.

Of course, there is nothing to stop a children's group meeting on a Sunday afternoon or a weekday evening. It helps the leadership problem a great deal, but it still leaves the question of what to do with the children while their parents are worshipping on Sunday morning. Mind you, there is nothing to stop adult Christian education being moved to a weekday evening either, freeing Sunday morning for joyous and serious all-age worship every week of the year!

Children are important in church. However, they are not more important than adults — all are equally important. In a world of compromise it is not true that the children's work must always adapt itself to fit around the adults' work, but neither is it true that the adults must always make sacrifices to allow the children's work to take place. Somewhere between the two is a least worst solution!

# Recruiting new leaders

In my own church I have seen every conceivable method of recruiting leaders used — personal invitations, open mornings where interested people can watch what happens without obligation, requests for volunteers, duplicated letters, emotional appeals, threats to close a department, and, in one memorable case where a young man who was ideal for the work refused to believe it, coercion! I would guess that I have probably listed them in order of desirability, but I wouldn't deny the possibility of the Holy Spirit working through any of them.

It is certainly true that the Spirit works through human nature more often than he works despite it. Volunteering is not a prominent feature of the human condition, and most people leading children's work are doing so because they were asked personally, or because others recognized their talents when they thought themselves incapable. There is no need to be ashamed of that fact. To help bring the vision of the congregation and the will of the Holy Spirit into line, remember these few principles. Make details of the vacancies public as far in advance of their crisis-date as possible. Let the congregation know precisely how much commitment of time and worry is expected. Assure potential leaders of (and provide them with) the training they need. Encourage short- to mid-length terms of service, rather than dauntingly long periods. Above all, present the work with a high profile, so that people realize what a vital and rewarding aspect of church life it is.

Jesus was talking about mission when he described God as the owner of the harvest. 'There is a large harvest, but few workers to gather it in. Pray to the owner of the harvest that he will send out workers to gather in his harvest' (Matthew 9:38). Maybe I should have put that principle at the head of the list, not the foot.

# Things to do

1 Ask yourself whether you have the qualifications for a Sunday school leader listed as 'Absolute essentials'. They each require a straightforward 'yes' or 'no'. If the answer to each is 'yes', take time to give God the glory for that. If you answered 'no' to any, spend some time praying about whether you are in the right job.

2 Go through the 'Qualities that leaders should show'. Mark yourself out of ten for each quality. Make plans to do something about areas where your score was low.

3 Have you become aware of areas in which you still need more training? If so, make a note of them. Who will you ask for advice as to how to get the help you need? Put the needs in an order of priority, so that you do not get overwhelmed by the size of the task. Make a plan of action that you know you can achieve in the next six months.

# 15
# One last word before you go

Well now! Are you raring to go, or do you feel like giving up for good? In either case, a moment's reflection would help.

If children's work sounds enjoyable and easy, that is a great blessing from God, but do not ever forget the seriousness of the work. We are engaged in a spiritual battle, alongside and on behalf of the children in our care. For them, every single thing in life which is of any importance is at stake. Everything! Paul reminded the members of the church at Ephesus that living the Christian life is not just a game, for we are dealing with 'spiritual forces in the heavenly world, the rulers, authorities, and cosmic powers of this dark age' (Ephesians 6:12). It is a mark of God's goodness to us that working and playing with boys and girls is so rewarding, but don't forget that 'everything you do or say should be done in the name of the Lord Jesus . . . for Christ is the real Master you serve' (Colossians 3:17,24).

On the other hand, if the thought of facing the children again fills you with dismay, even armed with the skills and understanding that you have acquired from this book, then don't despair. The church in Corinth in AD 50 sounds as if it was a disaster – disorderly in worship, undisciplined, divided, sexually immoral, the leaders having lost control of the way of the services were run. Yet Paul was able to write to them, 'My dear brothers, stand firm and steady. Keep busy always in your work for the Lord, since you know that nothing you do in the Lord's service is ever useless.' (1 Corinthians 15:58). What encouraging thoughts!

It is certainly true that, although they do not guarantee an easy life, the way we prepare, take stock of what we do, and pray about our work, will affect the way the Holy Spirit is effective through us.

## Preparing

Sometimes the very simplest disciplines make a large difference to the 'success' of children's activities. I'm hesitant to give hard-and-fast rules, but I must admit that these have helped me greatly:

- Get ready several days in advance. That way you can be completely familiar with the material and confident about its relevance to the children by the time you meet them. You will have enough time to buy or borrow any extra equipment you need, or seek help from someone else. The time in hand will also allow you to change your mind about what is the very best option for organizing or adapting an activity, so you need not always settle for your first idea.

- Set aside the same time in each week to do your preparation. It could be a lunch hour, or part of a particular evening, or immediately after running the previous event, while the children are still on your mind. Whichever suits you best, put it in your weekly diary as priority — if you need to change the time occasionally, be sure that you reschedule it properly.

- Get enough sleep the night before! This may mean leaving a party before midnight, but being a Cinderella on Saturday night is a small price to pay to avoid being the Sunday School's ugly sister the following morning.

- Arrive well before the children do, so that everying you are going to use is set out and you do not suddenly need to sharpen pencils when you could be chatting with children. Experience helps all leaders to develop their own collection of trouble-saving preparations. Mine include putting bookmarks in the pages to which I am going to refer in my Bible, hiding the football under a coat until it is needed, pinning the running order on my sleeve, and providing an 'interest table' on which children can (and must!) put the distracting toys they have brought after they have been admired. What are yours?

## Taking stock

There are certain questions that you should ask yourself, or discuss as a group of leaders, every week and every year. It is only by this kind of evaluation that you can tell whether your Sunday School is serving a useful purpose.

### Every week

Examine at least some, preferably all, of these questions for about five minutes. The point is not to condemn yourself, but to improve what you do next time:

- What did the children enjoy most, and how can I use that again to promote learning about the Christian faith?
- Did the children show any evidence that they remembered the content of the Bible teaching? Could I have told the story better?
- Were the visual aids I used large enough and clear enough to hold attention?
- Could I have improved on the organization of the session? (For example, could the way the children moved from one activity to another be better organized?)
- During worship and prayer did I sense that the children meant the words and actions they were using, or should I seek other ways of making that time relevant and important to them?
- For what percentage of the time were the children listening passively and for what percentage were they doing

something creative or involving? Have I got the proportion correct?

- What practical difference could the session potentially have made to the daily lives of the children who took part in it? What difference do I assess that it will actually make? How do I account for the shortfall?
- Who was missing today and why? Who requires special prayer or contact during the week? Is there any child I did not get to talk to or with whom I have 'unfinished business'?

**Every year**
- Did we meet the specific objectives that we identified last year?
- Have we covered a suitable range of Biblical topics, worship and practical applications?
- In what way has each child developed, especially spiritually, during the last year in Sunday School?
- Have we offered a variety of activities or are there any ruts into which we have slid?
- Has the size of the group increased, decreased or stayed the same? Is this what we planned and are we content with it? Are we attracting the children we targetted?
- Do we know all we need to know about the way each child's life outside Sunday School has changed in the past year?
- Have we made useful links with all the other generations of Christians in the church?
- Is each leader fulfilled and content about his or her role and responsibility in the group over the last year? Is there any area in which further training woluld be useful? What is each leader's future on the team?

## Praying

In 1 Thessalonians 3:9, Paul gives us an excellent model on which to base our prayers for church members in our care. He wrote, 'Now we can give thanks to our God for you. We thank him for the joy we have in his presence because of you. Day and night we ask him with all our heart to let us

168

see you personally and supply what is needed in your faith.'
Translated into Sunday School terms, this might involve
committing yourself regularly to thank God for each child
by name, to pray for opportunities to develop your relationship with him or her, and to ask that you will be able to play
your part in meeting the spiritual needs that you perceive in
each individual. The same could also apply to each leader
with whom you serve.

Prayer is work — indeed, it is hard work! Effective prayer
is not rushed or offered grudgingly. If personal prayer is
being squeezed out of your preparation and evaluation, it
may be because you are setting yourself an over-optimistic
target. To make grand schemes of prayer, then fail to fulfil
them, only produces guilt and does the children no good.
Make plans that you know are possible, then stick to them.
Perhaps it would be wise to cut the quantity of prayer and
increase its quality. Rather than pray for every child in your
group every day, it may be more valuable to pray for one
child each day, working your way through a list and using as
much detail as you can. There are other ways to discipline
your prayer — some groups allocate a small number of
children to each leader, who is asked to oversee and pray for
those boys and girls in particular. The important factor is
not the method, but the certainty that prayer will take place.
Remember that you are not doing God any favours by praying
to him — you are simply availing yourself of a most remark-
able free offer, his constant willingness to help.

Obviously, you must also pray for yourself and for every
activity which you are going to lead. If you feel that you
cannot cope, then ask for God's strength. If you feel fed up,
then do not be afraid to tell God about it. If you feel elated,
then thank God for the success he has given you. If you feel
unsure about what to do, claim God's promise to give you
guidance. None of these are our duty, they are merely
wonderful opportunities to receive the same assistance that
Jesus was given when he was in identical moods (John
12:27–28, Matthew 26:36–39, John 17:1–8, Luke 6:12–13).

# The last gasp

People ask me, 'What would you most like to say to all the Sunday School leaders of the world?' It's the kind of naff question which is impossible to answer — like, 'Where do you get all your ideas?' The closest I can get to a sensible answer is that more than anything else I would like to say, 'Thank you.' The reason is that very often everyone else forgets to say it!

St Paul told the church in Thessalonica how they should treat those whose task it is to give 'guidance and instruction in the Christian life' — in other words, you! He wrote, 'Treat them with the greatest respect and love because of the work they do' (1 Thessalonians 5:12–13). This is just a faint reflection of the respect and love that God himself has for those who serve him. His 'thank you' is the greatest encouragement and the greatest reward of all.

## Things to do

1   Answer these questions. They need simple answers, but definite ones.
(a)  At what time in each week will you do your Sunday School preparation?
(b)  At what time will you arrive for each meeting of the group?
(c)  At what time in each week will you answer the questions given in 'Taking stock'?
(d)  What date are you going to put in your diary as the day when you will review the past year's work, using the questions given?
(e)  What scheme of regular prayer for the children, leaders and yourself are you planning to follow?
(f)   To whom are you going to lend this book?

# Afterword

Seven years ago, ten-year-old Paul came into my classroom in tears. His dog had been rushed to the vet after being hit by a car, and he didn't know what to do. We talked about it, then prayed about it. Just the three of us — God, me and Paul. Over the years, we have talked and prayed a great deal more as I have watched him grow from a child who liked Bible stories into a man whose commitment to God means more to him than anything else.

This year I took him as a first-time leader on a children's Christian holiday. At one point during the week, a young boy came into the dormitory in tears. I immediately moved to help, but Paul was closer, and they went off together to talk about it, then pray about it. My first reaction was frustration because I thought I would be able to handle the situation better. Then it dawned on me that what was happening was precisely what I had prayed for and laboured for over seven years. The Christian boy had started to take on the work of the Christian man. That's how it is and that's how it should be! Just the three of them — God, Paul and a little child in tears! That's why this book is dedicated to him.

And me? I'm a very happy man!

# Resource list

**To give you the resources you need to run children's work in a church, week in, week out:**

*Learning Together with Under 5s* (with *Beginners* leaflets) Scripture Union, quarterly.

*Learning Together with 5–7s* (with *Friends of God* leaflets, Scripture Union, quarterly.

*Learning Together with 7–11s* (with *Adventurers* leaflets), Scripture Union, quarterly.

*Learning Together with 11–14s* (with *Lazer* magazine), Scripture Union, quarterly.

*Learning All Together — adults and children in church*, Scripture Union, quarterly.

**To help you think through what the Bible and experts in child development say about children:**

*Children Finding Faith*, Francis Bridger, Scripture Union, 1988.

*Children in the Way*, General Synod Board of Education, Church House Publishing, 1988.

*Children in the Worshipping Community*, David Ng and Virginia Thomas, J. Knox Press, 1986.

*Children and God*, Ron Buckland, Scripture Union, 1988.

*Parent's Guide 5–11*, Roger Owen, Kingsway, 1988.

**To inspire you to develop an all-age dimension to your church's life:**

*Learning All Together*, Scripture Union, quarterly.

*Know How to Encourage Family Worship*, Howard Mellor, Scripture Union, 1984.

*Know How – All-age Activities for Learning and Worship*, Michael Lush, Scripture Union, 1984.

*Using the Bible — with All Ages Together*, Donald and Patricia Griggs, Bible Society, 1983.

*Family Ministry*, Joe Leonard, Scripture Union, 1988.

*Welcoming Children to Communion*, Daniel Young, Grove, 1986.

**To help you present the Bible visually and dramatically, rather than academically**:
*Using the Bible — with Children*, David B. Hall, Bible Society, 1983.
*Help, I Can't Draw*, Sheila Pigrem, Falcon, 1977.
*Show Me!*, Julie Gattis Smith, Bible Society, 1985.
*Know How to Teach Every Child in Sunday School*, Douglas Sherburn, Scripture Union, 1979.
*Know How to Use an Overhead Projector*, Stephen H. Clark, Scripture Union, 1985.

**To help you worship alongside children:**
*Sing to God*, Scripture Union, 1971
*Praise God Together*, Scripture Union, 1984.
*Junior Praise*, Marshall Pickering, 1985.
*Junior Praise — Prayers and Readings*, Marshall Pickering, 1986.
*Church Family Worship*, Hodder and Stoughton, 1987.
*All-age Worship*, Maggie Durran, Angel Press, 1987.

**To give you creative ideas:**
*Infant Crafts*, Colin Caket, Blandford Press, 1983.
*Know How to use Art in Worship*, Valerie Bennett, Scripture Union, 1985.

**To enable you to encourage children to read the Bible regularly**:
*Quest* (for 7–11s), Scripture Union, quarterly.
*One to One* (for 10–13s), Scripture Union, quarterly.

**To get you enthusiastic for having fun**:
*Over 300 Games for all Occasions*, Patrick Goodland, Scripture Union, 1979.
*Over 120 Quizzes for all Occasions*, Rachel Green, Scripture Union, 1980.
*Know How — Special Events for all the Church Family*, Michael Lush, Scripture Union, 1986.

**To help you to talk to children who are considering committing themselves to Christ:**

*Jesus Loves Me*, Scripture Union, 1984.

**To challenge the way you think about churches and children in urban areas:**
*Faith in the City*, The Archbishop of Canterbury's Commission on Urban Priority Areas, Church House Publishing, 1985.
*Gutter Feelings*, Pip Wilson, Marshall, Morgan and Scott, 1985.

**To prepare you to run a holiday club:**
*Know How to run a Holiday Club*, David Savage, Scripture Union, 1986.
*Secret Agents*, Ron Fountain, Scripture Union, 1987.
*Scarecrows*, Peter Graystone, Scripture Union, 1988.
*The J Team*(for children with no Christian background), Peter Graystone, Scripture Union, 1989.
*Light Factory*, Janet Morgan and Angela Flynn, Scripture Union, 1991.


# Resources and training opportunities in Australia and New Zealand:

*New Zealand* National Office, 9a Oxford Terrace, Newtown, Wellington. Phone: 85 0485

*Australia* National Office, 241 Flinders Lane, Melbourne, Victoria 3000. Phone: 650 3733

*Queensland* 36 Agnes Street, Fortitude Valley 4006. Phone: 854 1658

*New South Wales* P O Box 93, Flemington Markets 2129. Phone: 746 2144

*Australian Capital Territory* Unit 5, Block 2, Shopping Centre, Cook 2614. Phone: 251 3677

*Victoria* P O Box 10, Richmond 3121. Phone: 417 4633

*Tasmania* 121 Bathurst Street, Hobart 7000. Phone: 34 2577

*South Australia* 28 Croydon Road, Keswick 5035. Phone: 371 0811

*Western Australia* P O Box 135, Mt Lawley 6050. Phone: 271 0066

*Northern Territory* P O Box 39164, Winnellie 0821. Phone: 48 0250

## Learning Together

Please send details and samples of Scripture Union's 'Learning Together' scheme of quarterly resource magazines for ministry among children and adults in churches.

I am particularly interested in material for:

Under 5s ......................    Name ..............................

5–7s ..............................

7–11s ............................    Address ..........................

11–14s ...........................    .........................................

Over 14s ........................    .........................................

Adults ...........................    .........................................

All-age services .............    Postcode ........................

Send to: *Help! There's a child in my church*!
Education in Churches department
Scripture Union
130 City Road
London
EC1V 2NJ